THE LOST ART OF READING

THE LOST ART OF READING

BOOKS AND RESISTANCE IN A TROUBLED TIME

DAVID L. ULIN

SASQUATCH BOOKS
SEATTLE

Printed in the United States of America
Published by Sasquatch Books

22 21 20 19 18   9 8 7 6 5 4 3 2 1

The Lost Art of Reading is based on an essay that appeared in the *Los Angeles Times* on August 9, 2009.

Other material in this book originally appeared, in significantly different form, in the *Los Angeles Times*, *LA Weekly*, *Columbia Journalism Review*, *Bookforum*, and the website ZinkZine. Some material in the introduction and the afterword was first developed in essays for the *Literary Hub*, the *Los Angeles Times*, and *Nieman Storyboard*.

A portion of the proceeds from the sale of this book will go to Sea Change Leadership PAC (www.seachangepac.org), a political action committee working to support the resistance movement and progressive candidates for office.

Editor: Gary Luke | Production editor: Bridget Sweet
Cover design: Anna Goldstein | Interior design: Bryce de Flamand

Cover photograph: © iStockPhoto.com | RG-vc

Library of Congress Cataloging-in-Publication Data
Names: Ulin, David L., author.
Title: The lost art of reading : books and resistance in a troubled time /
    David L. Ulin.
Description: Second edition. | Seattle, WA : Sasquatch Books, [2018] | Based
    on an essay that appeared in the Los Angeles Times on August 9, 2009.
Identifiers: LCCN 2018014337 | ISBN 9781632171948 (Hardcover)
Subjects: LCSH: Books and reading—Psychological aspects. | Information
    society. | Literature—Philosophy. | Ulin, David L.—Books and reading. |
    BISAC: LITERARY CRITICISM / Books & Reading. | LITERARY COLLECTIONS /
    Essays. | POLITICAL SCIENCE / Essays.
Classification: LCC Z1003 .U45 2018 | DDC 028/.9--dc23
LC record available at https://lccn.loc.gov/2018014337

ISBN: 978-1-63217-194-8

Sasquatch Books | 1904 Third Avenue, Suite 710 | Seattle, WA 98101
(206) 467-4300 | SasquatchBooks.com

For Rae, Noah, and Sophie

. . . you are the fire that will always burn . . .

ACKNOWLEDGMENTS

Even the most personal book is an exercise in collaboration, but *The Lost Art of Reading* has been more collaborative than most. I first developed the ideas here in an essay for the *Los Angeles Times*, where I had the privilege and the pleasure of writing about books for many years. I'd like to thank the *Times* for allowing me to pursue these passions . . . but most of all, I'd like to thank my editor there, the incomparable Orli Low, for making me a better writer by always pushing me to question my assumptions and dig more deeply into the material.

The Lost Art of Reading would not exist without Gary Luke at Sasquatch Books, who approached me about expanding my original essay and then gave me the space and breadth to do the work. Nor would it exist without my agent, Bonnie Nadell, who is, as she has always been, a voice of reason and support. Mark

Haskell Smith, Carolyn Kellogg, Dinah Lenney, Fred Mills, Matthew Zapruder, and Maret Orliss all helped, at various points, with ideas and inspiration; their voices, too, inform the book. Then, of course, there's my wife, Rae Dubow (*light of my life*, to steal a line from Nabokov), without whom none of this would matter; our daughter, Sophie, perhaps the most vigorous reader in the family; and our son, Noah, who once again has graciously allowed me to evoke him in a book.

As I worked on *The Lost Art of Reading*, I became aware of just how long I've been thinking about these issues and what, exactly, reading means to me. That should be obvious, I suppose, but it's amazing how much we take for granted, especially when it comes to what we love. Indeed, one of the finest rewards of this project was the opportunity it afforded me to collaborate with the writers I've revered across a lifetime, all the work that continues to mean so much to me. This book, then, is their book also, an expression of the back-and-forth, the ongoing conversation, that resides at the heart of how and why we read.

For this new edition, I added an introduction and afterword that seek to contextualize (if not make sense of) my earlier thinking in light of current events. Once again, I'd like to offer my gratitude to Gary Luke and Bonnie Nadell for their help in the preparation of this material, as well as Jonny Diamond at the *Literary Hub*, Susan Brenneman at the *Los Angeles Times*, and Kari Howard at *Nieman Storyboard* for encouragement and editorial intervention, as well as fellowship in these dark and disturbing days.

If everybody was silent for a year—if we could just stop this endless forward stumbling progress—wouldn't we all be better people? I think probably so. I think that the lack of poetry, the absence of poetry, the yearning to have something new, would be the best thing that could happen to our art. No poems for a solid year. Maybe two.

—Nicholson Baker, *The Anthologist*

INTRODUCTION
THE NECESSARY NARRATIVE

E arly in May 2017, the Transportation Security Administration initiated a pilot program at two domestic airports in which travelers were told to remove "paper products"—books, notebooks, and other documents—from carry-ons before X-ray screening. I know: at this point, when the news cycle seems to have sped up as if through time dilation, that reads like ancient history, especially since less than two months later, the TSA announced that testing had been completed and there were "no intentions of instituting those procedures" nationwide. All the same, bear with me, because suspended or otherwise, such a program has something to tell us about who and where we are. In the first place, the TSA may not have been true to its word, exactly; this past September, in Orlando, the agency released a statement affirming "new procedures" for travelers "to divest their electronics larger than a cell phone, liquids, and other items that may give a cluttered image to the X-ray operator. The other items can include food, books, and magazines."

More to the point, we've been here before. In October 2001, the American Library Association announced its opposition to the Patriot Act, particularly Section 215, the so-called "library records provision," which required librarians to turn over the records of patrons when asked to do so by law enforcement. That provision was sunsetted out of existence in 2015, but the aftereffect lingers like (to borrow a phrase from Don DeLillo) an airborne toxic event. "Censorship is never over for those who have experienced it," Nadine Gordimer once observed. "It is a brand on the imagination that affects the individual who has suffered it, forever." What she's describing is a state of fear. Something similar might be said in regard to the TSA, which is not in the business of security so much as it is in the business of "security theater": "a form of 'magical thinking,'" Bruce Schneier, a fellow at Harvard University's Berkman Klein Center for Internet & Society, has written, that "relies on the idea that we can somehow make ourselves safer by protecting against what the terrorists happened to do last time." Schneier's right. There is no point, no value, in making travelers take off their shoes because one time, a lone individual tried to blow up an airplane with a sneaker bomb. In the United States, however, we have lost the thread of logic in the stories that we tell. Just think about the headlines during the first twelve months of the Trump administration: the Muslim ban and the immigration raids, the Russia collusion investigation, the pussy-grabbing and the paid-off porn star. Just think about the racist rhetoric that runs, like excrement, from the president's mouth. On the one hand, America has always been a racist country. On the other, that has never before been rendered as acceptable. No, we are in the midst of a broken story, and we have lost the ability to parse its lines. Stories, I've long believed, are connective, the only tool we have to reach out of our isolation, regardless of how fleetingly. This is as close as I get to faith, this notion that narrative can save us, even (or especially) if we cannot, finally, be saved. And yet, living in this place and time, I wonder whether that's another disrupted narrative. What if stories are not what we need, not what brings us together, but rather, as Schneier asserts, "what we fear"?

Let's stay with that line of thought for a moment, because stories can be dangerous things. Those white supremacists in Charlottesville, with their Tiki torches and their khakis, were telling a story I would have thought we'd put behind us, until the election of 2016 made me realize how naïve I'd been. It's not that I believed racism, supremacy, had been vanquished; how could I, in a nation where, according to the *Guardian*, African American men between fifteen and thirty-four were nine times more likely to be killed by police in 2016 than other Americans? This is the narrative (or one of them) the supremacists and neo-Nazis sought to embody in Virginia: "You will not replace us," they chanted as they marched. The phrase derives from a 2012 book by the French writer Renaud Camus called *Le Grand Remplacement*, which argues that Europe is being "reverse colonized" by immigrants of color, a clash of civilizations that amounts to an existential threat. "People," Camus told the *New Yorker* in 2017, "are not just things. They come with their history, their culture, their language, with their looks, with their preferences. . . . The very essence of modernity is the fact that everything—and really *everything*—can be replaced by something else, which is absolutely monstrous." This is a ridiculous narrative, but it has staying power, going back to Cain and Abel, Exodus. What do we do with those we label *other*? For Camus, as for those in Charlottesville, the answer is simple: get rid of them. Here, we see the story trumpeted by the president from the first day of his campaign, and if you don't think that's important, consider the permission it bestowed, for instance, on James Alex Fields Jr., who killed thirty-two-year-old Heather Heyer and injured dozens of others when he drove his car into a crowd of counterprotesters. "I can't remember a bleaker time in this country's history," Charles P. Pierce lamented in *Esquire* the day after Heyer's murder. "The most perilous moments of the Cold War were frightening but, by and large, we were all in it together. The Vietnam period was angry and divisive but there was a central focus to all the rage, an ill-conceived and immoral foreign adventure that even its most wrathful opponents knew had to end some-time. But the centrifugal forces seem stronger and more mysterious this time. They seem to be coming from too many different directions and they seem to have a num-ber of obscure and distant sources. Our sense of being a self-governing nation is being pulled apart. Our concept of a political commonwealth is unmoored and floating. Nothing is solid. Everything is fluid, and everything ought not to be. Not like this. Not in the 21st century. We settled some things in the last century that should have been settled for good."

Pierce is referring to the collapse of collective nar-rative, which is what we are experiencing as a culture: left and right relying on their own news sources, Raw Story and the Daily Caller, MSNBC and Fox News. Not only that, but even the factions are factionalized, and have been since at least the 1960s. Purity, the rabid fervor of the true believer (the same for all extremists, left and right), versus pragmatism, competence. I have been on both sides, and I cannot say what I now believe. Instead, I have only stories. Such as: eighteen years ago, I cast my vote for Ralph Nader, in a state, California, that no Republican had won since 1988 and that Al Gore took by nearly 12 percentage points. Such as: eighteen years ago, I could still tell a classroom full of students that I might find common ground with, say, an evangelical from St. Louis, as long as we zeroed in on a few basic issues: housing and education and health care. At the same time, I have come to recognize that all these narratives are incomplete and every one turns out to be unfulfilling, because none of them add up to a vision larger than themselves. That's the problem in a nutshell, the betrayal of a certain promise, a faith in (let's call it) progress, that there is more that will unite than will divide us, whatever those terms have come to mean. And yet, I'm not so sure I share such a faith any longer—or that there is a faith to share. Last winter, not long after the inauguration, I moved for four months to Las Vegas, which means I spent a lot of time driving through the rural West. Every few weeks, I would return to Los Angeles to see my wife and children: four hours, 273 miles through the Mojave, the Angeles National Forest, Primm, Baker, Barstow, Victorville, Ontario, like a lost verse from a pop song about the open road. This, too, is a story, or perhaps more accurately several stories. "We were somewhere around Barstow on the edge of the desert," Hunter S. Thompson begins *Fear and Loathing in Las Vegas*, "when the drugs began to take hold." Whatever these towns may once have been, they are now roadside stops like any other, fast-food joints and outlet malls, snacks and cigarettes and gas. The great American homogenization, in which chains and cheap construction have yielded a landscape where towns appear interchangeable, although beneath their bland and echoed surfaces, I'm sure, beat distinct and differentiated hearts.

The first time I made this drive—or one like it— was in 1968, on a family trip. I was not quite seven years old. Just past Barstow, we made the turnoff for Interstate 40, passing first through Needles, California, then Arizona; we would take three weeks to travel east. Then as now, we were a nation divided, as we were once more in the 1980s, when I traversed these roads again. For hundreds of miles, radio gave up only farm reports and God talk, and when I stopped to eat or sleep or fill the tank, I was never unaware that I was a stranger in a strange land. "You a Jew, boy?" someone once asked in a small town in South Texas, and although he wasn't exactly threatening (more curious, I want to tell you), there was a moment when I wasn't sure how to respond. Still, how strange could this land be if it were also so accessible, so available to me? I-40, for instance: it would carry me across New Mexico into the Texas Panhandle, Oklahoma, Arkansas, Tennessee. I-15, were I to stay on past Las Vegas, would eventually bring me to Salt Lake City, Butte. There used to be a mileage sign in Wilmington, North Carolina, not far from I-40's terminus; "Barstow, Calif. 2,554," it declared. You might read that sign as information or as metaphor, but for me it was an emblem of the commons, of the country as a landscape we all share. Three decades later, in that same small town in Texas, I found myself at a 7-Eleven that had not been there the first time, in line between a teenager in board shorts, immersed in his phone, and a mother with three young kids. The scene was familiar, similar to what I might encounter in Santa Monica or suburban Boston: homogenization or progress, take your pick. I don't mean to make too much of this, except to acknowledge that I was mistaken, but I can't stop coming back to it, as well. "A story can take you through a whole process of searching, seeking, confronting, through conflicts, and then to a resolution," Maxine Hong Kingston writes in *The Woman Warrior*, and not unlike her, this is the narrative I want to share.

And yet, every narrative is conditional—isn't that what reading has to tell us? Every narrative is a slice of a larger whole. "All stories, if continued far enough, end in death," Ernest Hemingway notes in *Death in the Afternoon*, "and he is no true-story teller who would keep that from you." He's right, although it is also the case that most stories *don't* continue far enough, which means we have no choice but to engage with them as part of a continuum. Those narratives, they exist on either end of the page, before the action opens and after it is done. The fullest characters are the ones we can imagine walking around in the world. I think of Lucia Berlin and Tillie Olsen, of Grace Paley and Gina Berriault. "Listen, my dear alones," the latter implores us in the deft and brilliant "Women in Their Beds," "over there across the city. Do you remember how each time you lay yourself down in a bed you wondered, if even for a moment, what you were doing there? And what about the beds you thought you'd chosen yourself? Do they seem now chosen for you? Destiny's hand patting them down." This is a description not of closure but rather of closure's opposite—which is the existential tension (or one of them) at the heart of literature, the illusion that narrative can offer fulfillment when fulfillment is, at best, a fleeting reverie. As readers, then, we occupy an ongoing state of suspension. As readers and as humans, too. "In this world," Zadie Smith wrote not long after the 2016 election, "there is only incremental progress. Only the willfully blind can ignore that the history of human existence is simultaneously the history of pain: of brutality, murder, mass extinction, every form of venality and cyclical horror. No land is free of it; no people are without their bloodstain; no tribe entirely innocent. But there is still this redeeming matter of incremental progress. It might look small to those with apocalyptic perspectives, but to she who not so long ago could not vote, or drink from the same water fountain as her fellow citizens, or marry the person she chose, or live in a certain neighborhood, such incremental change feels enormous."

What Smith is addressing is an essential conundrum: we can live only in our own time. Even more, we cannot take anything for granted; it may be true, as Martin Luther King Jr. averred in a February 26, 1965, sermon at Temple Israel of Hollywood, that "the arc of the moral universe is long but it bends toward justice," yet such a process is neither passive nor foregone. King gave his sermon only a few weeks before Selma, tracing his own moral arc across the span of the Edmund Pettus Bridge. The march he led continued from

Montgomery to the Voting Rights Act, signed into law in August of the same year. In every way that matters, this too is a narrative, one that stands in opposition to that of Charlottesville. Indeed, it is the very narrative the neo-Nazis sought to erase or to invalidate there, that white supremacists (and their enablers) seek to invalidate still. I think about this all the time now, in a culture where the blurring of boundaries, the subjectivity of perspective, have become weaponized. I am a relativist —moral, aesthetic, intellectual. I don't believe in the innate authority of anything. And yet, what do I do with a society that appears to have slipped the bounds of reason altogether, in which a sizable percentage of the population is willing to believe, say, that collusion is a deep state conspiracy, or that, during her tenure as secretary of state, the most recent Democratic nominee for president approved a pay-to-play deal to transfer uranium to a Russian mining company called Uranium One? That none of this is true, that none of it ever happened, is, of course, beside the point. "Fake news," the president intones even as he pursues it like a piece of public policy. "I believe the state should be resisted wherever it encroaches," Denis Johnson argues in his 1995 essay "The Militia in Me," written in reaction to the bombing of the Alfred P. Murrah Federal Building in Oklahoma City. "But the bombers of that building will demonstrate for us something we don't want demonstrated: There's no trick to starting a revolution. Simply open fire on the state; the state will oblige by firing back. What's harder is to win a revolution, and the only victory worthy of the name will be a peaceable one."

So how do we win this peaceful revolution? How do we maintain a resistance worthy of the name? More useful, perhaps, to ask how we can take our division, our collective breakdown, and uncover, within or without it, a narrative that speaks to hope and not to fear. "This banality of violence," Ta-Nehisi Coates insists early in *Between the World and Me*, "can never excuse America, because America makes no claim to the banal. America believes itself exceptional, the greatest and noblest nation ever to exist, a lone champion standing between the white city of democracy and the terrorists, despots, barbarians, and other enemies of civilization. One cannot, at once, claim to be superhuman and then plead mortal error. I propose to take our countrymen's claims of American exceptionalism seriously, which is to say I propose subjecting our country to an exceptional moral standard. This is difficult because there exists, all around us, an apparatus urging us to accept American innocence at face value and not to inquire too much." I love this because of what it asks of us: not to dismiss the facile promise of exceptionalism but to take our rhetoric at face value and construct from it some sort of criterion—a national ethics, if you will. Responsibility, in other words, the responsibility of a nation that has never accepted its responsibility, that continues to believe it is, despite the evidence, golden and God blessed. "A shining city on a hill," Ronald Reagan called the United States in a speech the night before he was elected president, citing the Puritan John Winthrop, who as governor of the Massachusetts Bay Colony in the 1630s and 1640s opined that "a democracy is, amongst most civil nations, accounted the meanest and worst of all forms of government." Like Reagan, Winthrop understood the political necessity of narrative: "The eyes of all people," he said in his 1630 sermon "A Model of Christian Charity" (from which the "shining city on a hill" reference is also taken), "are upon us. So that if we shall deal falsely with our God in this work we have undertaken, and so cause him to withdraw his present help from us, we shall be made a story and a by-word through the world." At the same time, it is useful to read between the lines a little, if only to recall that, three months before his "city on a hill" speech, Reagan invoked states' rights during a campaign stop at the Neshoba County Fair in Philadelphia, Mississippi, where sixteen years earlier, three civil rights workers, James Chaney, Andrew

Goodman, and Mickey Schwerner, had been murdered by the Ku Klux Klan, whose members included officers of both the Neshoba County Sheriff's Department and the Philadelphia Police Department.

That this is all part of America, all part of the American narrative, should go without saying; history is meaningless if it is sanitized. At the same time, that history, that narrative, remains in flux, as narratives always are. There are no guarantees, no promises; progress, as Smith suggests, is incremental when it comes at all, and it can always be rolled back. Look at where we find ourselves, in the court of the crimson king. An example: forty-eight hours after the administration announced it would rescind temporary protected status for two hundred thousand Salvadorans in the United States, Immigration and Customs Enforcement agents raided 7-Elevens in seventeen states, arresting twenty-one undocumented workers. The next day, the president derided El Salvador, Haiti, and several African nations as "shithole countries" and wondered whether Nigerians lived in huts. This is, in the language of Joan Didion, "a different narrative altogether," although it is the narrative we have come to occupy. Even states' rights, long a dog whistle for white supremacists and racists, have lately taken on an altered resonance. "It's important, given these rumors that are out there, to let people know—more specifically today, employers—that if they voluntarily start giving up information about their employees or access to their employees in ways that contradict our new California laws, they subject themselves to actions by my office," California attorney general Xavier Becerra announced in January 2018, in response to the ICE raids. "We will prosecute those who violate the law." The law he was citing is the California Values Act, which effectively makes California a sanctuary state. That's a different story than the one told in the run-up to the Civil War, which involved the intention, by Southern states, to nullify federal laws (particularly involving slavery) they deemed unconstitutional. At the heart of this distinction is the issue of morality, which sits, as it must, at the center of every story. "The opinion that art should have nothing to do with politics is itself a political attitude," George Orwell argued in his essay "Why I Write," and this, too, is a concept I hold as something of a core belief.

I don't mean to trivialize our situation by referring to it through the lens of narrative, but rather to contextualize. This is how the world works: first we tell ourselves a story, then we dream our way inside it as a way of bringing it to life. It's why we have to be careful about the narratives we evoke or create, because they are bound by (or they bind) the limits of what we can imagine, the limits of our ability to think. The reason books and reading remain essential is because they are still the most effective mechanisms by which to crack open the universe. Think about it: when we read, we soul travel, in the sense that we join, or enter, the consciousness of another human. We empathize—we have to—because our experience is enlarged. "The purpose of literature," Reza Aslan wrote in 2011, "is to provide a window into other worlds." Only connect, in other words, which is, as it ever was, a key intent of narrative, although we must be willing to listen to one another for such a process to take hold. This is the problem with fake news, which has become pervasive precisely because it doesn't ask anything of us other than to have our preconceptions validated. We don't need to think or be confronted; all we need to do is be affirmed. Still, what is the purpose of news if not to inform us and, in so doing, stir us out of our complacency? The same, I want to say, applies to the whole art of writing, which involves asking questions that cannot be answered, embracing complexity. This is a difficult world, and I don't mean only in regard to policy, although many mornings, my news feed is too much to bear. It's a difficult world in which to be human, in which to try to live with integrity. That's what they're counting on, the purveyors of fake news as much as the politicians and the pundits, normalizing that which should not be normalized. It's not the facts that frighten them; facts, we all know, can be spun. It's the inquiry. Part of the intention is to shut down discourse, to appeal to our emotions rather than our minds. The more we react, the less we think. That's not conspiracy theory but simply circumstance.

Why do I read? I am looking for authority, intelligence. The last thing I want is someone to tell me what to think. But even more, perhaps, I seek engagement—with both the text and the creator of the text. I hesitate to make too much of this, because I also believe reading doesn't need to be prescriptive; it doesn't require any value other than itself. At the same time, how can it not also have a social function, since it grows out of a public, even a performative, act? "The relationship between public engagement and private thought are inseparable for me," Claudia Rankine has acknowledged. ". . . For me, there is no push and pull. There's no private world that doesn't include the dynamics of my political and social world. When I am working privately, my process includes a sense of what is happening in the world." A similar movement must take place in all of us. Faith again, some sort of transfiguration, the closest we come to real communion between ourselves and another who shares with us something in common (common cause, common courtesy, common knowledge, common sense). How could it be otherwise? We are all humans, lost on this green and dying planet, stumbling, alone together, in the dark. We must resist fear, not because there is some reward out there in the universe but because there is not. "Myths are made for the imagination to breathe life into them," Albert Camus—that other, better Camus, no relation to Renaud except for the name—writes in *The Myth of Sisyphus*; he is referring to resistance and responsibility. "If there is a personal fate," he continues, "there is no higher destiny, or at least there is, but one which he concludes is inevitable and despicable. For the rest, he knows himself to be the master of his days." Master of his days, or mistress, yes: it all begins with us. There is no one out there, no one coming to save us, no salvation really, if we are speaking existentially. We live; we die; it doesn't matter. The world will go on after we're extinct. There is only now, this moment, built on the succession of other moments, the long line of language and of history, humans talking to one another, generation after generation, from out of the depths of our loneliness and solitude. Tragic? Maybe, although I don't think so. "If this myth is tragic," Camus concludes, "that is because its hero is conscious."

And consciousness is what we now require, perhaps as much as ever—the space to sit in silence and to think. We need what I once called a quiet revolution, to resist the lures of clickbait and of gossip, to stand clear of all the fake news and the bots. A decade ago—or almost—when I first began to notice my distraction, I did not think of it entirely in political terms. I'm not so sure I do now either, although the lines have been more starkly drawn. Why does reading matter? Because language and narrative are what we have. Without them, we are just scared mammals reacting to the world around us, devoid of agency, of thought, betraying the necessary (and, yes, frightful) inheritance of our own consciousness.

Once, during a long-gone summer in another century, I made a trip to Europe with my girlfriend. I have written about this but not all of it; I found so many books there, I had to buy a suitcase in London to get them home. The flight to the United States was uneventful. I remember it, as I remember most long airplane trips, through the filter of what I was reading. Philip Norman's book of rock 'n' roll short stories, *Wild Thing*; Caroline Blackwood's bitter pill of a novel, *The Stepdaughter*. In the customs hall in Philadelphia, an officer asked me to open my bag. I had layered the top with dirty underwear, the kind of insignificant rebellion I favored at twenty-three. If someone was going to look through my things, I wanted to make it unpleasant or at least uncomfortable. I wanted him to wish that he were wearing gloves. As for the rest, it was just a gesture, since I had not brought anything restricted back. Yet here is what I've never told, although it seems to me, at this juncture, to be the most important part. The customs agent asked some questions about what I'd been doing while I was gone. Then, as he began to realize that my bag was full of paperbacks and hardcovers, he looked at me in another way. "What are you doing with all these books?" he asked, in a tone I recall as lightly menacing, although who knows, really, what he meant. It was almost the exact midpoint of the Reagan administration, less than three months before the 1984 election. In Europe, Americans were sewing Canadian flags to their backpacks; the week we returned, during a sound check for his weekly radio address, the president joked, "My fellow Americans, I'm pleased to tell you today that I've signed legislation that will outlaw Russia forever. We begin bombing in five minutes." (The audio clip later inspired a collaboration between Jerry Harrison, of Talking Heads, and Bootsy Collins: a one-off single called "Five Minutes," credited to Bonzo Goes to Washington.) What made me recoil was the idea—no, the implication—that books or reading could be dangerous. And yet, would we want it any other way? This is why I was drawn to them, because of what they taught, the doors they opened, what they allowed or encouraged me to see. In that bag was work by Amos Tutuola and Malcolm Lowry, Warren Miller's *The Cool World*, Sadegh Hedayat's *The Blind Owl*. In that bag were the mile markers of a road map I am still compiling, from one book to another and finally back to me. I remember standing on my side of a long table, facing that customs officer, uncertain of both his question and my response. Had I done anything wrong? How many books is too many? It felt as if he were insinuating something, but I couldn't say for sure. The answer, I should have told him, is that there can never be enough. Why should we fear one another's stories? The true act of resistance is to respond with hope. All those voices are what connect us. In a culture intent on keeping us divided, they are, they have been always, the necessary narrative.

Los Angeles, California
February 2018

One evening not long ago, my fifteen-year-old son, Noah, told me that literature was dead. We were at the dinner table, discussing *The Great Gatsby*, which he was reading for a ninth-grade humanities class. Part of the class structure involved annotation, which Noah detested; it kept pulling him out of the story to stop every few lines and make a note, mark a citation, to demonstrate that he'd been paying attention to what he read. "It would be so much easier if they'd let me *read* it," he lamented, and listening to him, I couldn't help but recall my own classroom experiences, the endless scansion of poetry, the sentence diagramming, the excavation of metaphor and form. I remembered reading, in junior high school, *Lord of the Flies*—a novel Noah had read (and loved) at summer camp, writing to me in a Facebook message that it was "seriously messed up"—and thinking, as my teacher detailed the symbolic structure, finding hidden nuance in literally every sentence, that what she was saying was impossible. How, I wondered, could William Golding have seeded his narrative so consciously and still have managed to write?

How could he have kept track of it all? Even then, I knew I wanted to be a writer, had begun to read with an eye toward how a book or story was built, and if this was what it took, this overriding sense of *consciousness*, then I would never be smart enough.

Now, I recognize this as one of the fallacies of teaching literature in the classroom, the need to seek a reckoning with *everything*, to imagine a framework, a rubric, in which each little piece makes sense. Literature—at least the literature to which I respond—doesn't work that way; it is conscious, yes, but with room for serendipity, a delicate balance between craft and art. This is why it's often difficult for writers to talk about their process, because the connections, the flow of storytelling, remain mysterious even to them. "I have to say that, for me, it evolved spontaneously. I didn't have any plan," Philip Roth once said of a scene in his 2006 novel *Everyman*, and if such a revelation can be frustrating to those who want to see the trick, the magic behind the magic, it is the only answer for a *writer*, who works for reasons that are, at their essence, the opposite of schematic: emotional, murky, not wholly identifiable—at least, if the writing's any good. That kind of writing, though, is difficult to teach, leaving us with scansion, annotation, all that sound and fury, a buzz of explication that obscures the elusive heartbeat of a book.

For Noah, I should say, this was not the issue—not on those terms, anyway. He merely wanted to finish the assignment so he could move on to something he preferred. As he is the first to admit, he is not a reader, which is to say that, unlike me, he does not frame the world through books. He reads when it moves him, but this is hardly constant; like many of his friends, his inner life is entwined within the circuits of his laptop, its electronic speed and hum. He was unmoved by my argument that *The Great Gatsby* was a terrific book; *yeah, yeah, yeah,* his hooded eyes seemed to tell me, *that's what you always say.* He was unmoved by my vague noises about Fitzgerald and modernity, by the notion that among the peculiar tensions of reading the novel now, as opposed to when it first came out, is an inevitable double vision, which suggests both how much and how little the society has changed. He was unmoved by my observation that, whatever else it might be, *The Great Gatsby* had been, and remains, a piece of popular fiction, defining its era in a way a novel would be hard-pressed to do today.

This is the conundrum, the gorilla in the midst of any conversation about literature in contemporary culture, the question of dilution and refraction, of whether and how books matter, of the impact they can have. We talk about the need to read, about reading at risk, about reluctant readers (mostly preadolescent and adolescent boys such as Noah), but we seem unwilling to confront the fallout of one simple observation: literature doesn't, *can't*, have the influence it once did. For Kurt Vonnegut, the writer who made me want to be a writer, the culprit was television. "When I started out," he recalled in 1997, "it was possible to make a living as a freelance writer of fiction, and live out of your mailbox, because it was still the golden age of magazines, and it looked as though that could go on forever. . . . Then television, with no malice whatsoever—just a better buy for advertisers—knocked the magazines out of business." For new media reactionaries such as Lee Siegel and Andrew Keen, the problem is technology, the endless distractions of the internet, the breakdown of authority in an age of blogs and Twitter, the collapse of narrative in a hyperlinked, multi-networked world. What this argument overlooks, of course, is that literary culture as we know it was the product of a technological revolution, one that began with Johannes Gutenberg's invention of movable type. We take books and mass literacy for granted, but in reality, they are a recent iteration, going back not even a millennium. Less than four hundred years ago—barely a century and a half after Gutenberg—John Milton could still pride himself without exaggeration on having read every book then available, the entire history of written thought accessible to a single mind. When I was in college, a friend and I worked on a short film, never finished, in which Milton somehow found himself brought forward in time to lower Manhattan's Strand bookstore, where the sheer volume of titles ("18 Miles of Books" is the store's slogan) provoked a kind of mental overload, causing him to run screaming from the store out into Broadway, only to be struck down by a New York City bus.

Milton (the real one, anyway) was part of a lineage, a conversation, in which books—indeed, print itself—made a difference in the world. The same might be said of Thomas Paine, who in January 1776 published *Common Sense* as an anonymous pamphlet and in so doing lighted the fuse of the American Revolution. Colonial America was a hotbed of print insurrectionism, with an active pamphlet culture that I imagine as the blogosphere of its day. Here we have another refutation to the antitechnology reactionaries, since one reason for print's primacy was that it was on the technological cutting edge. Like the blogs they resemble, most pamphlets came and went, selling a few hundred copies, speaking to a self-selected audience. *Common Sense*, on the other hand, became a colonial bestseller, racking up sales of 150,000; it was also widely disseminated and read aloud, which exposed it to hundreds of thousands more. The work was so influential that Thomas Jefferson used it as a template when he sat down a few months later to write the Declaration of Independence, distilling many of Paine's ideas (the natural dignity of humanity, the right to self-determination) in both content and form.

Given this level of saturation, it's not hard to make a case for *Common Sense* as the most important book ever published in America, but from the vantage point of the present, it raises questions that are less easily resolved. Could a book, any book, have this kind of impact in contemporary society? What about a movie or a website? Yes, the Daily Kos and FiveThirtyEight. com attracted devoted and obsessive traffic in the lead-up to the 2008 presidential election, but the percentages (and the effect) were nowhere near what Paine achieved. Even Michael Moore's film *Fahrenheit 9/11*, released barely six months before the 2004 election to packed theaters and impassioned public debate, came and went in the figurative blink of an eye. Partly, that's because Moore is a propagandist and Paine a philosopher; the key to *Common Sense* is the elegance of its argument, the way it balances polemic and persuasion, addressing those on both sides of the independence issue, always careful to seek common ground. Yet equally important is the speed and fragmentation of our public conversation, which quickly moved along to Swift Boats and other issues, leaving Moore behind. By November, *Fahrenheit 9/11* was little more than an afterthought, and six years later, if we remember it at all, it's as a dated artifact, a project whose shelf life did not even last as long as the election it sought to change.

This, in an elliptical way, is what Noah was getting at. How do things stick to us in a culture where information and ideas flare up so quickly that we have no time to assess one before another takes its place? How does reading maintain its hold on our imagination, or is that question even worth asking anymore? Noah may not be a reader, but he is hardly immune to the charms of a lovely sentence; a few weeks after our conversation at the dinner table, he told me he had finished *The Great Gatsby* and that the last few chapters had featured the most beautiful writing he'd ever read. "Yes, of course," I told him, pleased at the observation, but I couldn't help thinking back to our earlier talk about the novel, which had ended with Noah standing up and saying, in a tone as blunt as a lance thrust: "This is why no one reads anymore."

"What?" I said. He was back to talking about the annotation, but there was something else, a subtext to his words.

"This is why reading is over. None of my friends like it. Nobody wants to do it anymore."

He held my gaze for a long moment, as if challenging me to make a counterargument. Briefly, I thought about responding, but there was nothing to say. On the one hand, this was the primal conflict, my son declaring his independence, telling me that reading didn't matter in a room full of books, *my books*, thousands of them on the shelves. I almost asked for a towel to clean up the blood.

And yet, for all that I could recognize the dynamic, I found myself unsettled in another way. Yes, Noah was reacting; yes, he was putting me in my place. What I hadn't expected, though, was that as he left the room, I would be struck by a disturbing realization, one that spoke to the essence of who I was. *Literature is dead*, Noah had told me, *this is why reading is over*. And indeed, I saw now with the force of revelation, I could not say that he was wrong.

Sometime in the last few years—I don't remember when, exactly—I noticed I was having trouble sitting down to read. That's a problem if you read, as I do, for a living, but it's an even bigger problem if you read as a way of life. Since the moment I discovered literature, I've surrounded myself with books; every room, office, or apartment I've ever occupied has had its walls, floors, tables, nearly all available surfaces, covered with the effluvia of print. *Since the moment I discovered literature?* No, not even: before I would have thought to call myself a reader, books were as essential to me as air. I grew up in a house full of them, and among my earliest memories is one of scaling the floor-to-ceiling shelves in my parents' apartment on the Upper East Side of Manhattan to search out volumes with engaging cover illustrations, at which I'd stare for hours, trying to imagine myself into the scenes they portrayed. At the time, I couldn't have been older than six or seven, and the images that attracted me were those that mixed history and adventure, the fantastic and the real. I remember being struck by an old Bantam paperback novel about Genghis Khan, which featured a painting of the Mongol leader on horseback, at the head of a regiment of troops. Although I never did read the novel (nor develop a taste for historical fiction), I still recall the joy of contemplating that portrait, the way it made me feel as if a world had opened up in the palm of my hands. It is this, I think, that draws us to books in the first place, their nearly magical power to transport us to other landscapes, other lives.

For a long time, I read for just that reason, as if books were ripcords, escape hatches, portals out of my own life. I carried them with me everywhere: school, sleepovers, vacations, quick rides on the subway—any unattached moment, any place or piece of time. The summer I turned thirteen, in 1974, I spent a miserable two weeks holed up in a bunk at a Vermont tennis camp, wearing the same clothes every day, talking to no one, reading Roth and Bernard Malamud, neither of whom I fully understood. (The book I truly loved that summer was *Killer: Autobiography of a Mafia Hitman* by the pseudonymous Joey, a mob assassin who recounted, in glorious textured detail, the saga of his thirty-eight kills. I also loved watching an older girl with long brown hair dance alone to "I Saw Her Standing There" in the camp rec room after dinner one July evening, her body glowing in the fading dusk light, sinuous yet at once somehow still.) I was drawn to books that were beyond me; not all that many months later at a family Thanksgiving, I found myself digging through Robert Daley's *Target Blue*, a six-hundred-page account of the author's year as a New York deputy police commissioner. I spent the long gray afternoon and evening tuning out the brittle clannic gossip, ignoring the tensions, all those unfulfilled resentments, to see instead how many pages I could put away. Partly, this was emblematic of a false sophistication, a desire to shed the adolescent's greasy skin. I was not particularly good at being a thirteen-year-old (is anyone?), and I longed to be part of the adult world, a world I only dimly understood. Yet even more, I've come to think, it had to do with reading as a matter of imaginative or emotional reinvention, less a way out of my circumstances than a way out of *who I was*. What I was after, in other words, was not merely an escape but also a point of entry, a passport, or a series of passports, not to an older version of myself but to a different version—to the person I wanted to become.

In his 1967 memoir *Stop-Time*, Frank Conroy recalls a similar experience. Here's how he describes his own initiation into literature as a high school kid on the Upper East Side:

> Night after night, I'd lie in bed, with a glass
> of milk and a package of oatmeal cookies
> beside me, and read one paperback after
> another until two or three in the morning.
> I read everything, without selection, buying
> all the fiction on the racks of the local
> drugstore—D. H. Lawrence, Moravia, Stuart
> Engstrand, Aldous Huxley, Frank Yerby,
> Mailer, Twain, Gide, Dickens, Philip Wylie,

Tolstoi, Hemingway, Zola, Dreiser, Vardis
Fisher, Dostoievsky, G. B. Shaw, Thomas
Wolfe, Theodore Pratt, Scott Fitzgerald,
Joyce, Frederick Wakeman, Orwell,
McCullers, Remarque, James T. Farrell,
Steinbeck, de Maupassant, James Jones,
John O'Hara, Kipling, Mann, Saki, Sinclair
Lewis, Maugham, Dumas, and dozens more.
I borrowed from the public library ten blocks
away and from the rental library at Womrath's
on Madison Avenue. I read very fast,
uncritically, and without retention, seeking
only to escape from my own life through the
imaginative plunge into another. Safe in my
room with milk and cookies I disappeared
into inner space. The real world dissolved
and I was free to drift in fantasy, living a
thousand lives, each one more powerful,
more accessible, and more real than my own.

Look at that list—at the glorious, indiscriminate
range of it—and you begin to see something essential
about how (certain) adolescents read. Even more, you
get a whisper of the power of books to change us, to
alter our emotional DNA. The key is to think about

reading as a journey of discovery, an excavation of the inner world. It doesn't matter whose, exactly—not yet, anyway. What's important is to take the plunge. You could argue that the immersion Conroy details in this passage is superficial, that his scattershot approach, of devouring *everything* (a random tactic if ever there was one, less about intention than availability), of reading "very fast, uncritically, and without retention," is antithetical to the interior connections he seeks. But more accurate, I'd suggest, is that for Conroy, reading is a way of mapping the territory and that what he's revealing here are the first tentative steps toward building a frame. Conroy was not my contemporary; he was born in 1936, the same year as my father. Yet from the moment I discovered *Stop-Time*, in the spring of 1977, when I was a sophomore at a New England boarding school, I felt as if I were in the presence of an alter ego, whose existence was not unlike my own. There was the profound explication of otherness, of observing as opposed to living fully in the world. There was the early, and abiding, awareness of mortality, the consciousness "of ourselves as pinpoints of life in a world of dead things, impurities that sand, coral, water, and dead mules were only tolerating." There was, of course, the Upper East Side, a landscape Conroy had inhabited much as I did, wandering the same streets, going to the same movie theaters, taking the same subways: reading him, I could almost see the heat rising from the sidewalks, in shimmering waves of refracted light.

Where it all came together was in the reading, that accidental mix of authors, that sense of books as a retreat. Most striking about Conroy's list is how similar it is to what I was reading at the same age, even down to Philip Wylie (*Philip Wylie?*), who is, I must imagine, wholly unremembered, despite having written the 1940s bestseller *A Generation of Vipers* and the novel *When Worlds Collide*. For me, the books of Wylie's that resonated were *The Smuggled Atom Bomb* and *The Spy Who Spoke Porpoise* (both of which I bought, in fifth or sixth grade, at a school used-book sale), even though, like Conroy, I read them quickly and recalled nothing, so that I could not say now what either is about. Yet here's what I do remember: Wylie had a niece who was murdered, with her roommate, in their apartment on the Upper East Side. This was in 1963, before the boot-up of my conscious memory, but for some reason— perhaps because the killings had taken place in the neighborhood, or maybe because they had inspired the pilot of the TV series *Kojak*, which I watched with an attentive devotion—they echoed for me with an unlikely vibrancy.

At the heart of this was an intimation that for all their outside status, writers, or writing, did not exist apart from the world but rather in it, that in language, narrative, literature, I might find the substance of an interaction far more complex and enduring than mere escape. I can't explain it exactly, other than to say that such a perception wasn't overt, that it was something I was beginning, on the vaguest level, to feel instead of know. Had anyone asked about it, I wouldn't have known what they meant, but all these years later I see the roots of a deeper reckoning with literature, the first inkling of the idea that in their intimacy, the one-to-one attention they demand, books are fundamentally about engagement, that they require a context, that they reflect a writer's place, his or her standing, a situation *and* a story. It's no coincidence that Conroy ends his reverie on reading by admitting, "It was around this time that I first thought of becoming a writer. In a cheap novel the hero was asked his profession at a cocktail party. 'I'm a novelist,' he said, and I remember putting the book down and thinking, my God what a beautiful thing to be able to say." Yes, indeed, a beautiful thing: to enter into that conversation, not just to map the territory, but to participate in its creation as well.

This, of course, is what readers, as well as writers, do—participate, be part of the back-and-forth, help bring the text to life. Kurt Vonnegut once described literature as the only art in which the audience plays the score, and if that's a bit of a throwaway, it's also astute. Reading is an act of contemplation, perhaps the only act in which we allow ourselves to merge with the consciousness of another human being. We possess the books we read, animating the waiting stillness of their language, but they possess us also, filling us with thoughts and observations, asking us to make them part of ourselves. This, too, is what Conroy was getting at, the way books enlarge us by giving direct access to experiences not our own.

I might have read carelessly as a kid, but I also read deeply, obsessively—personalizing, even fetishizing, the books I cared about. In junior high school, I arranged my library (already, I was not just a reader but a collector, my own floor-to-ceiling shelves stretching across one long wall of my bedroom) according to preference, with my favorite authors—Vonnegut and Mario Puzo, but also Roth, E. L. Doctorow, Joseph Heller . . . see what I mean about liking books that were beyond me?—on a shelf in the center of the wall, everything else radiating outward from that core. In my mind, this was the library as virtual city, a *litropolis*, in which the further you were from the axis, the less essential a story you had to tell. To populate this city, I bought books at sales and in secondhand shops, by writers I often didn't know: Conor Cruise O'Brien, Sam Greenlee, L. Fletcher Prouty, Richard Condon, R. V. Cassill, Robert Rimmer, Frederick Forsyth, Ladislas Farago. Some of them I read (Rimmer's *The Harrad Experiment* was, for obvious reasons, an adolescent favorite, as was Greenlee's *The Spook Who Sat by the Door* and Prouty's *The Secret Team*, both of which helped catalyze a growing sense of political anxiety, further fueled by the Watergate scandal and a Super 8 copy of the Zapruder film that I had ordered for twenty dollars out of the back of *Argosy* magazine), and some I never got to. But there they were, all of them, on those shelves together, my attempt at mapping the literary city in my mind. Although I don't want to make too much of this, looking back I can't help but see it as a strategy for turning concrete something that might otherwise have remained the most elusive of abstractions, as if only by thinking metaphorically might I take my interests, tastes, desires, even my aspirations, and make them three-dimensional and solid in the world.

This suggests another set of tensions, between ideas and action, but maybe it's the source of a strange kind of reconciliation as well. For many years, I

physicalized (there's no other word for it) my reading, understanding cities by their bookstores, recalling trips in terms of what I'd read. The summer
after graduating from college, my girlfriend, Rae, and
I backpacked through Europe, she visiting museums
as I drifted from bookshop to bookshop, buying everything I couldn't get in the States: a Penguin UK edition of Thomas Mann's *Joseph and His Brothers*, Pan
and Panther paperbacks of Philip K. Dick and Thomas
M. Disch novels, even *Tom Sawyer Abroad* and *Tom
Sawyer, Detective*, together in a single beat-up volume,
which I picked up for a couple of francs at Shakespeare
and Company on the Left Bank. Part of the appeal was
the stores themselves—the stores as landmarks, the
stores, I may as well admit it, as holy sites. That's how
I felt about the Strand, or San Francisco's City Lights,
as if I were in the presence not only of books but *literature*, an endless human conversation going back to the
beginning of recorded language, Homer and the Bible
blurring into Vonnegut, Heller, Roth, Mann, even
Puzo: all of them the pieces of an enormous mashup,
ongoing and unbounded, reaching beyond the bor-
ders of a single life. The sensation was animal. I would
walk into a favorite bookstore, Spring Street Books in
lower Manhattan, say, and just the sight, the smell, the
breadth of all that writing, lining the walls and piled

on the frontlist tables, would hit me in the bowels. All of a sudden, my stomach would roll and my sphincter would tighten, and I would feel an urgency that was physical and metaphysical, an expression of my body and my mind. I loved that feeling, loved how it made me quicken, loved the sense that I was sinking—or no, not sinking but immersing, immersing in the very lineage Conroy had described. Even to think about it now is enough to make me feel it, although Spring Street Books has been gone for close to fifteen years. It's the same feeling I have sometimes in my own home, looking for a book on the shelves, tracing my finger along all those spines, all those reflections, all those stories that both add up and never add up, all the refraction and the residue.

In Europe, I ended up with so many books I had to buy a suitcase to bring them home. After we landed in Philadelphia, a U.S. Customs officer asked what I had left the country for. How could I explain that the answer was right there, in that suitcase, that if for Rae the highlight of the trip had been the older man in Florence who had offered us a personal tour of the Uffizi (shades of Ian McEwan's *The Comfort of Strangers*, which I also bought, and read, that summer), for me it had been the unlikely coincidence of stumbling across a London bookstall once owned by the Scottish novelist Alexander Trocchi, whose work, then as now, I revered. Trocchi Rare Books, it was called—nearly twenty-six years later, I still carry the business card in my wallet—in the antiquarian market on King's Road, and I came away with a signed paperback of the author's 1960 antimasterpiece *Cain's Book*, as well as a green Olympia Press Traveller's Companion edition of the fifth volume of Frank Harris's *My Life and Loves*, which he had cranked out in 1954 for Olympia publisher Maurice Girodias in a celebrated literary hoax.

Trocchi was, at the time, a new fascination, made more alluring by the fact that, except for *Cain's Book* and the 1954 novel *Young Adam*, an existential thriller in which a Glasgow barge worker allows an innocent man to hang for a murder he knows he didn't commit, it was impossible to find his books. This, undoubtedly, was a function of the marginal nature of so much of his writing, which included a collection of poems called *Man at Leisure*, a handful of translations, and a series of so-called *dbs*, or dirty books, that he had written for Girodias in the mid-1950s as works-for-hire. Yet even more, I think, Trocchi's magnetism had to do with the unrelenting fierceness of his aesthetic, which occupied a territory beyond conventional morality, where notions such as right and wrong, guilt or innocence, were

merely "convenient social fictions[s]" and the responsibility of the artist was to exist inviolable and apart. "It
is necessary only to act 'as if' one's conventional catego-
ries were arbitrary to come gradually to know that they
are," he declares in *Young Adam*, and both the best of
the *dbs* (*Thongs*, *White Thighs*, *Helen and Desire*) and
Cain's Book (it's not called that for nothing) echo this
uncompromising point of view. As Trocchi writes in
the closing lines of that novel: "Ending, I should not
care to estimate what has been accomplished. In terms
of art and literature?—such concepts I sometimes read
about, but they have nothing in intimacy with what I
am doing, exposing, obscuring. Only at the end I am
still sitting here, writing, with the feeling I have not
even begun to say what I mean, apparently sane still,
and with a sense of my freedom and responsibility,
more or less cut off as I was before."

What was the appeal of such a writer? In many
ways, he was, and remains, the natural endpoint of
the arc Conroy had begun. *Stop-Time*, after all, also
offers its own brand of nihilism, in its reflections
on mortality as well as its author's uneasy sense that
he, too, must always stand apart. The difference is
that, for Conroy, this was not so much a matter of phi-
losophy as one of personality, less thought out than
felt. His book is framed by two brief sections recalling

drunken late-night drives through the English coun-
tryside; the second ends with him puking in a fountain
after losing control of his car and slamming into a low
curb. "I was going to die," he reflects, as the accident
unravels. "As the fountain grew larger I felt myself
relax. I leaned toward the door. Let it come. Let it
come as hard and fast as it can. Touch the wheel, make
an adjustment so it will strike right beside me. Here
it comes! *Here it comes!*" What's compelling about
such a moment is its mix of exhilaration and resignation, the idea of looking annihilation in the face and
crying, *Bring it on*. It's foolhardy, full of false bravado
. . . and yet at the same time touched by the inevitable,
by an unblinking willingness to stare down the abyss.
When I first read *Stop-Time*, I found this so disturbing—the embrace of obliteration, the insistence that
we turn into the dark—that I couldn't make sense of
it. Why veer toward death when life was so fleeting,
why seek out extermination before it came? But in
many ways, that's what Trocchi is after also, although
his position is more intellectual than emotional: literature as ideological stance. In *Thongs*, which uses the
language of S&M to expose the hypocrisy of the bour-
geoisie, who pay lip service to conventional morality
while repressing their own shameful secrets and half-
articulated desires, Trocchi frames a trenchant critique

of "the tepid thing you call living," arguing that only by "rais[ing] passion to such a level that life becomes extinct within it" can we ever indulge our "lust for the infinite," although paradoxically, it will destroy us in the end.

Lest this come off as empty theorizing, Trocchi meant every word of it: by the time *Cain's Book* appeared, he was already a junkie, a condition the book celebrates as a philosophical choice. "I'm going to try / to nullify my life," Lou Reed sings in "Heroin," a song that may as well be channeling Trocchi, so similar is its nihilism, the belief that even the most authentic life is an act of capitulation, if only because of the brittle frailness of our mortal skin. After *Cain's Book*, Trocchi never finished another full-length piece of writing, dabbling with a project called *The Long Book*, agitating as part of the British anti-university movement of the 1960s, shooting heroin ("Trocchi believed he was so powerful, both in his mind and in his body," recalled his British publisher John Calder, "that he could resist anything, and of course he got hooked very quickly and was never able to get off it for the rest of his life"), and eventually losing everything he loved or cared about: his family, his art, his very self. It was, one imagines, a bitter solace to know that such loss comes to everyone, that it is the essential condition of humanity, this vaporous evanescence, this whittling away.

That, of course, was part of my attraction to Trocchi. At twenty-two, I was drawn to the extremists, and there was something brave, I thought (and think still), about his insistence to strip away every last piece of sentimental reaction, even as he recognized the impossibility of the task. Reading Trocchi was like watching an existentialist rewrite the Four Noble Truths of Buddhism—1) Life is suffering; 2) The origin of suffering is attachment; 3) The cessation of suffering is attainable; 4) There is a path out of suffering, the Nobel Eightfold Path—as if he were the bastard son of Jack Kerouac and Albert Camus. Like the former, he got sidetracked by the first truth and bogged down in the second. Like the latter, he understood that the only true cessation of suffering would come from the cessation of consciousness. For Camus, such contradictions resolved themselves in an acceptance of absurdity: "One must imagine Sisyphus happy," he wrote. For Trocchi, that was not going nearly far enough. "You call life meaningless," he writes in *Thongs*, "and you think you assert your freedom in rejecting it. But your act of suicide is just as meaningless as any other."

This is what literature, at its best and most unrelenting, offers: a slicing through of all the noise and the ephemera, a cutting to the chase. There is something thrilling about it, this unburdening, the idea of getting at a truth so profound that, for a moment anyway, we become transcendent in the fullest sense. I'm not talking here about posterity, which is its own kind of fantasy, in which we regard books as tombstones instead of souls. No, I'm thinking more of literature as a voice of pure expression, a cry in the dark. Its futility is what makes it noble: nothing will come of this, no one will be saved, but it is worth your attention anyway. And yet, for that reason, perhaps—and in much the same way as Conroy—Trocchi becomes the emblem of another, more fundamentally human conflict: that of the outsider who could not escape himself. Like all of us, he was never able to bypass the noise completely; he had to eat and sleep and pay his bills, to exist in three dimensions in the world. "Life is, in large part, rubbish," David Shields writes in his book *Reality Hunger*, by way of suggesting how quickly an existence "consecrated to art" wears thin. For Trocchi, this meant the rare book business, which is where I almost came face-to-face with him. I recall standing in the antiquarian market, surrounded by coin and jewelry dealers, asking the middle-aged book dealer if he knew Trocchi's work. He was tall, slightly heavyset, with a gray widow's peak and a tweed jacket—impeccably British, I would have described him, if I'd been thinking in such terms. At the mention of Trocchi's name, he smiled thinly, as if confirming something to himself. Then he asked if I knew the name of the bookstall, and when I told him that I didn't, he took that business card out of his jacket and handed it to me.

I want to tell you that it took me a minute to gather the pieces, that there was a flash of cognitive dissonance. Or no . . . maybe what I want to tell you is that I saw everything in an instant, as if I were watching a circle close. Either is possible; I don't know anymore. What I *do* recall was the look on the bookseller's face, expectant, and the way he said, as soft as an insinuation, "This is his stall."

"What?" I might have answered. Or: "No way." Or: "Oh my God." I know my body started racing, that I was aware of the boundaries growing porous, of being in the presence of a coincidence or connection bigger than I could fully comprehend. If this is how literature often made me feel, I wasn't used to facing it in three dimensions, other than my oddly visceral reaction to entering a bookstore, that pulsing in my guts and in my blood. I had come upon this place by accident, attracted by the shelves of old paperbacks, by their open-ended sense of chance. I had been looking, in a general sort of way, for books by Trocchi, but now, it seemed, I'd stumbled on a passage to the man himself. "Is he here?" I heard myself ask. "Can I meet him?" The man's face tightened, a creasing at the eyes, and I wondered if I'd crossed a line. I had the sudden realization that he was a caretaker, that his job was not only to sell books but also to deflect people like me. *Should I apologize?* I wondered, but before I could, he took my elbow in the gentlest possible manner, as if he were about to lead me somewhere—away from Trocchi, I supposed. Then, he leaned across the space between us, and in a voice halfway between a lamentation and a whisper, told me, "He died six weeks ago."

A quarter of a century later, the moment is still vivid. I remember standing there, buffeted by an almost physical sensation of a lost chance, of having come so close to something I didn't even know was possible until it was denied. And yet, that's not all of it, not exactly, for what would I have done had Trocchi been alive? What would I have said to him . . . and even more, what would he have said to me? Looking back, it is almost with a measure of relief—not that he was dead but that he was inaccessible—that there was no person to interfere with the idea of him I had built out of his books.

Here, we see the conundrum of the reader, the way the intimacy of words, of language, can't help but butt up against the unbridgability of personality or time. Over the years, I've met many of the writers whose work helped to transform me: Vonnegut, Roth, Heller, Allen Ginsberg, William S. Burroughs, Norman Mailer, Joan Didion. In almost every instance, it's been gripping, although even the best of these encounters has felt glancing when compared to the imminence, the interiority, of their books. Now, I take it for granted that the real relationship is not with the writer but with the writing, that it's on the page where we find the deepest sympathies. Still, for a long time, I sought echoes of these associations in the physical, if not between writer and reader then between a writer and him- or herself. In 1986, on a cross-country trip with Rae, I used Jack Kerouac's *On the Road* almost as a travelogue; there was something revelatory about reading it while watching the country change as it had for Sal Paradise and Dean Moriarty, "all that raw land that rolls in one unbelievable huge bulge over to the West Coast, and all that road going, all the people dreaming in the immensity of it." In North Platte, Nebraska—a desolate Plains town, industrial and flat, dust blowing off the river—I nodded at Kerouac's take on the place:

I felt something different in the air in North Platte, I didn't know what it was. In five minutes I did. We got back on the truck and roared off. It got dark quickly. We all had a shot, and suddenly I looked, and the verdant farmfields of the Platte began to disappear and in their stead, so far you couldn't see to the end, appeared long flat wastelands of sand and sagebrush. I was astounded.

"What in the hell is this?" I cried out to Slim.

"This is the beginning of the rangelands, boy. Hand me another drink."

This, I thought, was literature in three dimensions, the writing mirroring the grayness of the twilight and the town and the river, not to mention my own longing for Kerouac's resolution: "The great blazing stars came out, the far-receding sand hills got dim. I felt like an arrow that could shoot out all the way."

Two years later, I had a similar experience in Dollarton, outside Vancouver, British Columbia, where Rae and I, by then married, spent one day of our honeymoon visiting the beach on which Malcolm Lowry had lived for more than a decade with his wife, Marjorie, in a squatter's shack. We walked the trail he describes

in his late novella "The Forest Path to the Spring,"
"wandering along the banks of the inlet through snow-
berry and thimbleberry and shallow bushes, with the
sea below you on the right, and the shingled roofs of
the houses, all built down on the beach beneath round
the little crescent of the bay." We stood on the rocky
shore he had inhabited for so long in delicate suspension between transience and permanence and where no
trace of him—not a foundation footprint, not a piece of
driftwood—remained. Evanescence again, the press of
the void, the touch of futility. All had long been encoded
into my relationship with Lowry, who was, not unlike
Kerouac or Trocchi, another damaged visionary: an
alcoholic who never completed another book after the
1947 publication of *Under the Volcano* and who died in
1957, under unsettled circumstances, a month before
he would have turned forty-eight. What's interesting
about "The Forest Path to the Spring," though, is how
serene it is, and even more, how accurate in its description of place. Here's Lowry:

> If you can imagine yourself taking a pleasure
> steamer down the inlet from the city some
> afternoon, going toward the northern
> mountains, first you would have left the city
> harbor with its great freighters from all over

the world . . . and its shipyards, and then
to starboard would be the railway tracks,
running away from the city along the bank,
through the oil-refinery station, along the
foot of steep cliffs that rose to a high wooden
hill, into Port Boden, and then, curving out
of sight, beginning their long climb into
the mountains; on the port side beneath the
white peaks and the huge forestation of the
mountain slopes would be tide-flats, a gravel
pit, the Indian reserve, a barge company,
and then the point where the wild roses were
blowing and the mergansers nested, with the
lighthouse itself; it was here, once around
the point with the lighthouse dropping astern,
that you would be cutting across our bay with
our little cabins under the trees on the beach
where we lived at Eridanus, and that was our
path going along the bank.

Standing there, on Lowry's beach with Rae, looking out into the inlet, I could see it all, everything that
he had recorded more than thirty years before, as if
his prose had come to life. I can see the scene now, in
my mind, another quarter of a century later, the beach

curving like a scar along the water, the refinery station, the tideflats, the mountains rising up behind us, the stillness of the bay, the sunlight gentle on its surface, a caress. To this day, I've never again had this experience, to observe in three dimensions a place I'd read about and have it reflect, exactly, the image in my head. This is how good Lowry was, I remember thinking, and this is what language, at its most acute, can do. It can collapse the distances, bring us into not just the thoughts but also the perceptions of a writer, allow us, however fleetingly, to inhabit, literally, his or her eyes. Sure, it's an illusion, a trick of ink and paper; sure, all literature, all art, is a construction, a creation, flawed and flimsy, an attempt to rerender, in symbols, the substance of who we are. Still, there is a nobility to the gesture, not least because it is preordained to fail. This is what the postmodernists don't get, that if literature is a game, it is a game of serious consequences, in which we communicate across an irreconcilable divide. "Writing in silence, reading in silence," E. L. Doctorow once said of the peculiar isolated intimacy of the enterprise, and that, I think, is it precisely: the tension, the balance, the sense of being somehow within the world and at the same time without it, the push-and-pull between writer and reader, the unlikely process by which literature works.

It's been years since I came to books in such a way, seeking out the physical associations, trying to frame them in both time and space. And yet, the Upper East Side; North Platte, Nebraska; the beach at Dollarton; even, in some sense, Trocchi's London bookstall—all exist for me in parallel locations, as landscapes in the world and on the page. "I write entirely to find out what I'm thinking, what I'm looking at, what I see and what it means. What I want and what I fear," Joan Didion notes in her essay "Why I Write," and it's no understatement to suggest that this is what the dynamic between a writer and a reader offers from the other side as well. Or it was, at any rate, until the moment I became aware, in an apartment full of books, that I could no longer find within myself the quiet necessary to read.

When I say I can no longer find the necessary quiet, I am engaging, I'll admit it, in hyperbole. Or no . . . not hyperbole, but oversimplification, reduction, a way of building a frame around something that may resist the impulse to be framed. And yet, this, I think, is something on which we can agree: to read, we need a certain kind of silence, an ability to filter out the noise. That seems increasingly elusive in our overnetworked society, where every buzz and rumor is instantly blogged and tweeted, and it is not contemplation we desire but an odd sort of distraction, distraction masquerading as being in the know. In such a land-scape, knowledge can't help but fall prey to illusion, albeit an illusion that is deeply seductive, with its promise that speed can lead us to illumination, that it is more important to react than to think deeply, that something must be attached to every bit of time. Here, we have my reading problem in a nutshell, for books insist we take the opposite position, that we immerse, slow down. "After September 11," Mona Simpson wrote as part of a 2001 *LA Weekly* roundtable on reading in wartime, "I didn't read books for the news. Books, by their nature, are never new enough." Simpson doesn't mean that she stopped reading; rather, at a moment when it felt as if time was on fast forward, she relied on books to pull back from the onslaught, to distance herself from the present as a way of reconnecting with a more elemental sense of who we are.

If the source of my distraction is somewhat dif-ferent—not an event of great significance but the usual ongoing trivialities—the issue is not dissimilar, a fracturing of my concentration, a susceptibility to the tumult of the culture, to the blog posts and news updates, all the hue and cry. For most of my adult life, I have read, like E. I. Lonoff in Roth's *The Ghost Writer*, primarily at night: a hundred or so pages every evening once Rae and the kids have gone to bed. These days, after spending hours on the computer, I pick up a book and read a paragraph; then my mind wanders and I check my email, drift onto the internet, pace the house before returning to the page. Or I want to do these things but don't, force myself to remain still, to follow what I'm reading until I give myself over to the flow. What I'm struggling with is the encroachment of the buzz, the sense that there is something out there that merits my attention, when in fact it's mostly just a series of disconnected riffs, quick takes and fragments, that add up to the anxiety of the age.

How did this happen? Perhaps it's easier to pinpoint when. Certainly, it began after the fall of 2006, when I first got high-speed internet, which I had previously resisted because I understood my tendency to lose myself in the instant gratifications of the information stream. Certainly, the 2008 election kicked it into overdrive, since I spent much of that year hooked up to the electronic pipeline, checking news and analysis sites almost constantly, taking the temperature of the campaign. I have a mental picture of myself at the computer, several on-screen windows open, one an email queue, one a piece of writing, the rest digital shards of reportage or documentation from a variety of sources: CNN, Reuters, Fox. I know this is apocryphal because, even in this era of extreme distraction,

I am not a multitasker, but rather someone who does first one thing and then the next in scattered sequence, closing each application before opening another, looking, for the most part, at a single item at a time. And yet, something about this image strikes me with the force of metaphor, with the essence of emotional truth. It may not strictly be the case that I spent the ten and a half months from the Iowa Caucuses to the general election ping-ponging between competing news outlets, but that's the way I remember it. Every poll number, every shift in delegate counts and endorsements—it all felt so immensely freighted that to look back now is to recall little more than the frantic blur of stimulation, the lab rat's manipulated jolt at pressing the proper button, the junkie's temporary relief at the fleeting fix.

Partly, of course, that had to do with what was at stake in 2008. But even more, I think, the importance of the moment arose out of a feeling that we were at the tipping point of a collective breakdown, in which our sense of common narrative had become hopelessly frayed. If it seems odd to discover narrative disconnect in a campaign that seemed, at times, defined entirely in terms of story line, so be it: there's a difference between narrative and dramatic arc. Without question, the election had plenty of the latter, beginning with the simplest and most monumental—a primary battle between an African American and a woman, without a white man in sight. It's rare, in a culture as media managed as this one, to see something truly revolutionary, a harbinger of epic change. And yet, what was the flip side of that revolution? The manufactured posture of Sarah Palin, a public figure so empty and callow that she could not name the newspapers she did not read. For me, the election turned with her nomination, becoming a clash not just of competing ideologies but, yes, of *competing narratives*. For me, she, not John McCain, came to represent the anti–Barack Obama, the emblem of a vision so cynical that it would resort, without any sense of shame or history, to the tactics and language of the Bund. Here we were, in October, after McCain had tanked his response to the financial crisis, watching political rallies in which a major party nominee was derided as a traitor and a terrorist. Here we were, watching Palin supporters talk openly of armed rebellion, while the candidate did nothing to calm the tone. Perhaps the most chilling moment occurred in Minnesota on October 10, when McCain was booed at one of his own events for trying—too little too late— to bring an air of reason and civility back to the campaign. "I have to tell you," he reassured a man who had expressed fear of an Obama presidency, "Senator Obama is a decent person and a person you don't have to be scared of as president of the United States." When a woman declared that she couldn't trust Obama because he was an Arab, McCain corrected her, noting that the Democratic nominee was, in fact, "a citizen," and took the microphone away.

On the one hand, this is so ridiculous that it demeans the notion of a public discourse: an ignorance that transcends stupidity. At the same time, it speaks to a more comprehensive dissolution, in which the very idea of a common ground, or common narrative, has been rendered obsolete. "Atomization," Joan Didion calls it in her 1968 essay "Slouching Towards Bethlehem," which frames Haight-Ashbury during the Summer of Love as a metaphor for the collapse of . . . everything. "The center was not holding," Didion opens the piece:

> It was a country of bankruptcy notices
> and public-auction announcements and
> commonplace reports of casual killings and
> misplaced children and abandoned homes
> and vandals who misspelled even the four-
> letter words they scrawled. It was a country
> in which families routinely disappeared,
> trailing bad checks and repossession papers.
> Adolescents drifted from city to torn city,

sloughing off both the past and the future as
snakes shed their skins, children who were
never taught and would never now learn the
games that had held the society together.
People were missing. Children were missing.
Parents were missing. Those left behind
filed desultory missing-persons reports, then
moved on themselves.

Didion, here, is also being hyperbolic, although
her generalities (*families routinely disappearing, adolescents drifting from city to torn city*) point us to a
deeper truth. It may be, as she acknowledges, that this
"was not a country in open revolution," but if "the market was steady and the G.N.P. high and a great many
articulate people seemed to have a sense of high social
purpose," all that is beside the point. Instead, what she
is diagnosing is a social malaise, a cultural condition,
no less relevant to us now than it was forty years ago.
At the heart of the crisis is not just the evaporation
of what we once referred to as shared assumptions,
but even more, a dysfunction of language, a failure
of the tools of rhetoric and logic on which consensus
relies. "This was not a traditional generational rebellion," Didion writes about the kids who were drawn
to Haight-Ashbury in the spring and summer of 1967

like moths to an especially incandescent flame. "At some point between 1945 and 1967 we had somehow neglected to tell these children the rules of the game we happened to be playing. Maybe we had stopped believing in the rules ourselves, maybe we were having a failure of nerve about the game." Either way, she continues, "because they do not believe in words—words are for 'typeheads,' Chester Anderson tells them, and a thought which needs words is just one more of those ego trips—their only proficient vocabulary is in the society's platitudes."

As always with Didion, there's a sharp edge of class-consciousness, an innate conservatism, in the marrow of her argument. What does she mean by "the rules of the game we happened to be playing" if not the traditional narrative of the middle class? And yet, it would be a mistake to read this as mere lament, for Didion is smart enough to know that narrative has long since shattered, that the dissolution has its roots in the fall-out from the atom bomb. Hence, the casual reference to 1945 as a point of demarcation, since it was in the paired flashpoints of Hiroshima and Nagasaki that the notion of a central narrative went entirely off the rails. Hence, the emphasis on "atomization," since in the wake of those explosions all the verities society had for so long cherished—faith and family, status and achievement, a sense of shared identity—became the fractured pieces of a world on the brink of annihilation, no longer relevant except as a collective lie. "I want you to understand exactly what you are getting," Didion explains at the beginning of "In the Islands": "You are getting a woman who for some time now has felt radically separated from most of the ideas that seem to interest other people. You are getting a woman who somewhere along the line misplaced whatever slight faith she ever had in the social contract, in the meliorative principle, in the whole grand pattern of human endeavor. . . . I have trouble making certain connections. I have trouble maintaining the basic notion that keeping promises matters in a world where everything I was taught seems beside the point. The point itself seems increasingly obscure." In her 1991 essay "Pacific Distances," she frames the issue in more basic terms. "When I first moved to Los Angeles from New York, in 1964," she writes, describing her reaction to L.A.'s "tranced hours," its "seductive unconnectedness," "I found this absence of narrative a deprivation. At the end of two years I realized (quite suddenly, one morning in the car) that I had come to find narrative sentimental."

It is, for those of us who live in Southern California, tempting to read this as a matter of geography, which is, in part, what Didion intends. But it is equally the case that she is getting at something larger, at the way narrative can be manipulated, at the way narrative can deceive. This is the contemporary malaise, the malaise of the overlapping story, a malaise defined by the cacophony of voices, by the chaos, by the roar. We live in an era when everyone wants to tell his or her story, but there is no real sense of what story means anymore. Politicians appear on *The View* or *The Oprah Winfrey Show* to share their narratives, to highlight, in a succession of talking points, the epiphanies by which they came to understand the world. Fake memoirists such as James Frey or Peggy Seltzer devalue an entire genre by inventing new lives for themselves—lives that are, apparently, more "authentic" than the ones they have actually led. Reality TV blurs our sense of what *real* means; everyone survives on *Survivor*, after all. Meanwhile, the twenty-four-hour information cycle eats it all up, framing commentary as reportage and vice versa until we no longer know what is gloss and what is news. The result is a culture that is almost entirely mediated, although as David Shields points out in *Reality Hunger*, "*Reality*, as Nabokov never got tired of reminding us, is the one word that is meaningless without quotation marks."

As it happens, I agree with Shields—and with Nabokov too. Yet again, I think, it doesn't matter; I accept the idea of mediation, but I still want to be moved. Every dedicated reader is familiar with the idea of the living line, the sentence that seems to leap off the page in all its vibrating tension, as the author wrestles (*I write entirely to find out what I'm thinking*) with whatever he or she cannot quite know. "It's time to be blunt," Tim O'Brien admits in his 1990 book *The Things They Carried*, a work that blurs the line between fact and fiction, staking out a territory beyond either one. "I'm forty-three years old, true, and I'm a writer now, and a long time ago I walked through Quang Ngai Province as a foot soldier. . . . Almost everything else is invented." Here, O'Brien gets to the heart of the matter, the way the best stories can't help but surprise us, offering multiple answers, or no answers, resisting our attempts to encapsulate them, to render them in definitive form. "I want you to feel what I felt," he tells us. "I want you to know why story-truth is truer sometimes than happening-truth." And: "What stories can do, I guess, is make things present." Compare this with Jenny Sanford, betrayed first lady of South Carolina, who in her 2010 memoir *Staying True*—the title alone is a giveaway of her intentions—acknowledges no doubts, no questions, just a steely sense of self-determination, the belief that she has "given of herself . . . [and] worked on building character," that she bears no responsibility for her story, that it is merely something that happened to her.

If it seems unfair, holding Sanford up against O'Brien, let me offer this as a defense. Yes, the two books are different, with divergent purposes: the one an open-ended, private exploration, and the other an act of political manipulation, an attempt to frame a public point of view. Still, in the divide between them, we can begin to trace the boundaries of our cultural dislocation, the way we have lost touch with *narrative* in favor of the more amorphous notion of *narratives*. This is the sin of Frey and Seltzer—not that they lied but that they lied so badly, that their inventions were not in the service of any significant "story-truth." We come to books (or, at least, I do) to see beneath the cover story, to be challenged and confounded, made to question our assumptions, even as the writers we read are compelled to question their own.

What does that mean? On the one hand, it's an argument for nuance, for the role of narrative as a mechanism to confront the chaos, to frame a set of possible interpretations while acknowledging that these could shift at any time. Yet even more essential, I would argue, it's a call to engage. Stories, after all—whether aesthetic or political—require sustained concentration; we need to approach them as one side of a conversation in which we also play a part. If we don't, we end up susceptible to manipulation, emotional or otherwise. In February 1946, Hermann Goering told the judges of the Nuremberg tribunal, "Naturally the common people don't want war. . . . But, after all, it is the leaders of a country who determine policy, and it is always a simple matter to drag the people along, whether it is a democracy, or a fascist dictatorship, or parliament, or a communist dictatorship. All you have to do is tell them they are being attacked, and denounce the pacifists for lack of patriotism and exposing the country to danger. It works the same in every country." Such a statement is chilling on all sorts of levels, but nowhere more than in its recognition of the fact that we are complicit in our fate. It's not so far a leap to trace a line between Goering's sentiments and the most extreme attitudes of our own era, from Ari Fleischer's cautionary comment, in the aftermath of the destruction of the Twin Towers, that Americans "need to watch what they say, watch what they do" to the manufactured controversies of the Birthers and the 9/11 conspiracy theorists, who exemplify the idea that belief alone is now enough, in certain quarters, to give something the weight of truth. The effect might not be equivalent, but the implications are: that by not asking questions, by reacting rather than thinking, we allow ourselves to be susceptible to all manner of lies. Here we have the fallout from the detonation of the central narrative, the breakdown of a kind of collective dialogue, in which, in the name of some amorphous fantasy of identity or ideology, we succumb to the most reptilian of our fears.

This is what stories can stand against, if we approach them in a certain way. Again, Thomas Paine is instructive . . . the man who wrote the American narrative into being. In *Common Sense*, he builds a complex argument for independence (based on a layered critique of monarchy and the divine right of kings) around the most basic of issues: economics and security. Indeed, to read *Common Sense* now is to be amazed at its essential conservatism, at Paine's sense of America as not just a metaphorical Eden but also a resource to be exploited for financial and political gain. "Our plan is commerce," he writes, "and that, well attended to, will secure us the peace and friendship of all Europe; because, it is the interest of all Europe to have America a *free port*." And yet, if this is the hook—the carrot, as it were—he follows it up with a far more knotty stick. Paine knows independence is dangerous. He understands it will require an act of creativity so far-ranging as to be almost unimaginable: the construction of an entire country. Tellingly, he is vague on the details. "I only presume," he tells us, "to offer hints, not plans." The implication is that the particulars are for us to figure out. The same, I think, can be said of reading, in which we are given a template that we must remake as our own. Call it what you want, narrative or story-truth, but in the end, it is an act of creativity no less elusive than what Paine evoked, a way for us to understand ourselves.

I decided I would help Noah with *The Great Gatsby*. He didn't ask, not exactly, but neither did he say no. First, I showed him some of my annotations: a galley of a novel I was reviewing, the marked-up copy of a text I was preparing to teach. He stood just inside the door of my home office, thumbing through the pages, smiling closely. "You'd fail if you were in my class," he said.

Noah was right: I am a minimalist when it comes to marginalia . . . or maybe, it's just that I know what works for me. Either way, I've developed my own short-hand for note taking, a system of slashes and asterisks and underlinings that take the place of language, that serve more as memory triggers—*cite this*—than as the component parts of any intellectual or critical frame. It's not that I mind highlighting passages that move me; in fact, I've grown so used to reading with a pen in my hand that I miss it with an almost physical ache when I read for pleasure, as if in the act of annotation I can't help but take a deeper dive. And yet, like Noah, I don't want to be distracted, don't want to be pulled out of the flow. The sample annotations that he showed me—a series of page spreads covered with small, precise loops of writing—made my head hurt, not so much because of the denseness of the commentary as because of how it cluttered up the page. Too many notes can get overwhelming, interposing the reader's sensibility on top of the writer's until the latter is obscured. To me, this is antithetical to the nature of the process, which is (or should be) porous, an interweaving rather than a dissemination, a blending, not an imposition, of sensibilities.

I didn't say all this to Noah. Instead, I suggested a way to game the system by using a version of my shorthand as he was reading and then returning to fill out his comments afterwards. I also offered to reread the novel with him, so we could discuss it as he worked. He gave me a look, eyes skeptical, but again, he didn't turn me down. "How far are you into it?" I asked, and when he said his class had finished the first six chapters, I went to the shelves and took down my old Scribner paperback: the same copy I had read in high school, with that flapper face on the cover, outlined in the night above the gleaming chaos of electric lights, her sad eyes recalling the billboard of Doctor T. J. Eckleburg, who watches over the tumult of the novel with a gaze as disconnected and impassive as that of God. I paged through the book to see what I was looking at. One hundred eighteen pages, not a problem. I could do that in a couple of hours. It was a Sunday afternoon in March, and the rest of the day extended before me like a question mark. I talked to Noah for another minute before he went off to his room. From behind the closed door, I could hear music—Green Day, the soundtrack to *Rent*—and the sound of laughter as he iChatted with a friend. I took *The Great Gatsby* into the living room and stretched out on the couch. "In my younger and more vulnerable days," the novel opens, "my father gave me some advice that I've been turning over in my mind ever since. . . . 'Whenever you feel like criticizing anyone,' he told me, 'just remember that all the people in this world haven't had the advantages that you've had.'" There it was, right from the beginning, the classic Fitzgerald preoccupation with privilege and class. And then this: "He didn't say any more but we've always been unusually communicative in a reserved way and I understood that he meant a great deal more than that."

Unusually communicative in a reserved way. Here we had the essence of the father-son dynamic, evoked in less than a sentence, in six particularly well-chosen words. I felt a flash of recognition, of connection, felt myself slip beneath the surface of the language, felt the book rise up as if to swallow me. This was what I'd been missing, that full-bore immersion; this was what reading had to offer, that balance of first and second sight, of knowing and unknowing, of finding yourself in someone else. My initial response was one of relief, and not just because I'd slid into the book so easily. It had been decades since I'd read *The Great Gatsby*, and I hadn't known for sure how it would be. Rereading can be a tricky process, in which, for better or worse, you're brought face-to-face with both the present and the past. It's different than reading, more layered, more nuanced, with implications about how we've changed. In her 2005 book *Rereadings*, Anne Fadiman traces the distinction between reading and rereading: "The former had more velocity; the latter had more depth. The former shut out the world in order to focus on the story; the latter dragged in the world in order to assess the story. The former was more fun; the latter was more cynical. But what was remarkable about the latter was that it *contained* the former: even while, as with the upper half of a set of bifocals, I saw the book through the complicating lens of adulthood, I also saw it through the memory of the first time I'd read it." That was true, although those memories sometimes turned out to be deceptive; I had lost books by rereading them, Flannery O'Connor's *Wise Blood*, for instance, which I had loved in college but not so much later, when I began to see it as a young writer's pastiche, less about life as it really is than a naif's projection of how life might be. This was my worry with *The Great Gatsby*, which Fitzgerald wrote in his late twenties. (The book was published when he was twenty-nine.) How much could he have known, especially about his own vulnerability and failings, about the way the world can take everything from us, our pride, our aspirations, our very hearts? This was why I admired his later work—*The Crack-Up*, *The Pat Hobby Stories*, *The Love of the Last Tycoon*—because, flawed as it was, it revealed a Fitzgerald beyond the stereotype, a damaged man, older and more weighted. "I remember riding in a taxi one afternoon between very tall buildings under a mauve and rosy sky," he wrote in 1932, looking back at 1920, when *This Side of Paradise* had made him the toast of Manhattan. "I began to bawl because I had everything I wanted and knew I would never be so happy again."

Here we see the blending of the personal and universal, the way Fitzgerald's specific experience (*riding in a taxi one afternoon between very tall buildings under a mauve and rosy sky*) bleeds into a broader human understanding of loss. The longing is almost palpable, the sense that joy is fleeting, that even the most profound satisfactions (*I had everything I wanted*) must fade beneath the press of time. Could the younger Fitzgerald have recognized this? *The Great Gatsby* shows he did. When Nick leaves Gatsby's house for the first time, after a manic weekend party, he glimpses a similar sort of dissipation, the loneliness that comes encoded in the most frantic celebrations, the silence at the center of the world. "I glanced back once," he tells us. "A wafer of a moon was shining over Gatsby's house, making the night fine as before and surviving the laughter and the sound of his still glowing garden. A sudden emptiness seemed to flow now from the windows and the great doors, endowing with complete isolation the figure of the host who stood on the porch, his hand up in a formal gesture of farewell."

It's impossible to read these lines without thinking in some way of Fitzgerald himself. "Mostly, we authors must repeat ourselves—that's the truth," he acknowledged in a 1933 essay called "One Hundred False Starts," published in the *Saturday Evening Post*. "We have two or three great moving experiences in our lives— experiences so great and moving that it doesn't seem at the time that anyone else has been so caught up and pounded and dazzled and astonished and beaten and broken and rescued and illuminated and rewarded and humbled in just that way ever before." That's a great line, true of all my most iconic writers: Didion and Kerouac, Conroy and Trocchi, and, of course, poor Malcolm Lowry, sitting on his beach in British Columbia, trying to write his way out of alcoholism and defeat. But it may be truest of Fitzgerald, who has long been misread as a social chronicler, tagged, like Kerouac, with the awful burden of being labeled the voice of his generation, until the particulars of his fascination, those *two or three great moving experiences*, are subsumed by another kind of myth. I kept thinking about this as I read the first six chapters of *The Great Gatsby*, kept thinking about the architectures we erect over certain books and authors, until their essence is obscured. This, I would suggest, is another problem, the way we talk around rather than about the books we read, the way we tend to focus on everything except the thing itself.

And yet . . . as that long Sunday afternoon passed like liquid honey, I began to drift. Partly, it was the silence, as amorphous as time passing. Partly, it was the light, slow and diffuse. Partly, it was exhaustion, which kept rising up to infiltrate the lulling heartbeat of the words. But most of all, I must admit, it was distraction, an inability to hold at bay the insistence of the world. I read for a bit, then clicked on the television, checked the news from spring training, watched some forgotten film. I called Rae, who was out with our daughter, Sophie; I took the dog for a walk. I flipped ahead to see how many pages were in each chapter, as if to calibrate my experience. This is something I have always done, a way to position myself in a book. But such knowledge can be a two-way street, and on this Sunday it began to work against me, occasioning not anticipation but instead a kind of dread.

In the end, I forced myself to stick with the reading, if for no other reason than that I owed it to my son. I wanted to set an example, to be a role model—but also to come to his rescue, to swim out into the shifting currents of the novel and carry him home. I kept thinking about a trip we'd taken to Hawaii a few years earlier for a family vacation. Rae, Noah, and I decided to go scuba diving, off a boat that trolled the reefs not far from shore. We drove up in our shorts and sunscreen, met the other tourists, chatted briefly about how little we knew. I'd gone on a couple of dives as a teenager, in the gentle waters of the Caribbean; I had loved the experience of flying beneath the surface of the ocean, dipping and rising with a slight kick of my flippers, submerging, rolling, free of gravity, passing above schools of colored fish as if I were one myself. The water had been so warm I'd worn a bathing suit and T-shirt; it was, as I recalled, like immersing in a giant tub or pool. The first indication that this was going to be different came when the dive instructor laid several wetsuits across the aft deck and told us each to find one that fit. The second came as soon as we emerged from the chute of the harbor and turned into the open water of the Pacific. Immediately, we found ourselves buffeted by waves, pitched in sweeping rolls of water, although we were no more than a hundred yards off the coast. Rae was the first to succumb, before she could even get into a wetsuit; her face grew pale, her skin slickened, and then she was throwing up over the rail. She spent the rest of the morning lying on one of the benches that lined the mid-deck, face tucked into the crook of an elbow, eyes shut tightly against the rocking of the boat.

Noah and I fared better—initially, at least. ("Seasickness-wise," David Foster Wallace writes in his essay "A Supposedly Fun Thing I'll Never Do Again," "it turns out that heavy seas are sort of like battle: there's no way to know ahead of time how you'll react.") We got our wetsuits on, although the chop made balance difficult, and I could feel my stomach lurch. Off the stern, the ocean looked inviting, not just because it was cool and green but also because, the dive instructor kept telling us, once in it, we would be less susceptible to the way it moved. We went in as a group, and within a second I knew I was in trouble. The water was rough, up and down, up and down, a constant lapping. I put the rebreather in my mouth and slipped below the surface, but it was not much better underneath. I could feel the currents, their relentless pulling, could feel the tug of the mask on my face. I began to breathe quickly, as if at the edges of panic; instinctively, I broke for the reassurance of the air. The satisfaction was fleeting, since as soon as I came up I started bouncing. Water got in my mouth and nose. The boat was only a dozen feet away, an easy swim, but there was no comfort in that realization. Besides, my son was in the water, twenty or so feet down with the rest of the divers, and I had to keep an eye on him.

So I went back down into the water, back below the surface once again. I angled toward the others, who were in a cluster near a guide wire, some of the more adventurous already branching off for the jagged architecture of a nearby reef. Noah was easy to find—he was with the instructor, practicing navigation, the two of them swimming together nearly in mirror image, like an underwater *pas de deux*. I turned away, submerged a bit, swam off a little on my own. I was still breathing fast, but the panic had receded, leaving in its place a more general anxiety. This wasn't diving as I remembered it. This wasn't easy; this was a fight. The currents kept pushing me, first toward the shore, and then away; it was requiring all my stamina to stay in the general area of the boat. All of a sudden, I had a realization: I was, in the most literal sense imaginable, in over my head. Forty-six years old, out of shape, not the strongest swimmer, in waters more assertive than I had ever known. This is how people die, I remember thinking . . . and then I looked over to where Noah was still drifting and saw that something had gone wrong.

I watched him point to the surface, watched the instructor shake his head no, then watched a cloud of something (it looked like fish food, although I later understood that it was vomit) explode from Noah's mouthpiece as his body went slack. I turned and swam to them, moving as fast as the current would allow. I could feel my body start to rush with adrenaline, not a flood but a kind of steady growing tension, steeped not in panic but in fear. As I pushed through the tide, the instructor took my son's arm and began to lead him to the surface. I caught up with them just in time to watch Noah give a little shudder, as if he were coming awake. Behind his face mask, his eyes fluttered; I could see his chest move as the instructor held the mouthpiece to his lips. *Get him up, get him up*, I thought, taking Noah's other arm and rising with them. And then we broke through. The air was a revelation, the sky blue and unblinkered, the ocean bobbing beneath us, our bodies bouncing up and down like corks. I spit out my rebreather, took a long breath as I maneuvered behind Noah, let him recline against my chest. I wrapped an arm around his upper body to keep his head above the waves. The instructor pointed toward the boat, which was still close, although we had drifted: maybe ten, maybe fifteen yards. Then he asked if I would be all right without him, and when I nodded, he slipped back underneath the water and was gone.

And I know that there were other instructors watching. And I know that the crew of the boat was there to help. When I got Noah to the stern, only a minute or two after we had broken the surface, I was met by three men, all reaching out to grab his arms and legs, to help me raise him to the deck. Twenty minutes later, sitting on the deck myself, sipping from a bottle of water and looking at my wife and son, both now supine on those benches, sleeping off the experience as if it were a particularly nasty drunk, I could already see the contours of the story, could already sense the narrative it would become. But before it became a story, during that minute or two in the water, what I recollect most sharply is the sense that things could go either way. Ten or fifteen yards is a marathon when you're swimming against the current with another body in your arms, and it was in the last few feet, as we came up along the port side of the boat and had to turn to reach the diving platform, that I became truly terrified. In the movie *Jaws*—which I saw so many times as a thirteen-year-old that I can still quote large chunks of it verbatim—Robert Shaw, as Quint, recounts the saga of the USS *Indianapolis*, torpedoed in the Pacific on July 30, 1945, shortly after delivering components of the Hiroshima bomb. "Noon the fifth day, Mr. Hooper," he tells Richard Dreyfuss, "a Lockheed Ventura saw us, he swung in low and he saw us. He's a young pilot, a lot younger than Mr. Hooper, anyway he saw us and come in low. And three hours later a big fat PBY comes down and starts to pick us up. You know that was the time I was most frightened? Waiting for my turn. I'll never put on a lifejacket again."

Shaw's monologue gets it exactly right, the way I felt in the water also, my sense that if tragedy was coming it would be in these final seconds, that this was when eternity might bare its teeth. Although that didn't happen, in some odd fashion the feeling carried over, even after we got back to land. Two years later, listening as Noah complained about *The Great Gatsby*, I had a mental image of him floundering in the linguistic ocean of the novel, much as he had floundered in the Pacific on that diving day. I had the inspiration that I could come retrieve him, that together we could make it back to the boat.

Noah, of course, had other ideas. On Monday morning, while driving him to the school bus, I tried to talk about Fitzgerald, but he rebuffed me in the bluntest terms. "I've got it covered," he said, when I asked about his annotations, and when I pushed a little, bringing up the eyes of Doctor T. J. Eckleburg, he rolled his own eyes at me and shifted to face the window. "You know," I told him, "I spent the whole afternoon yesterday reading to help you." Even as I was speaking, we both recognized the emptiness of the guilt. Noah turned back toward me slowly, his gaze dark and indistinct. *Don't worry about it*, I almost said, *forget it*—but it was too late. If the art of parenting is, as I often think, the art of keeping your mouth shut, I had blown it. I had said too much.

And so I waited for Noah to deliver my comeuppance, in the way that only a fifteen-year-old can. When it came, it was surprisingly gentle:

"I didn't ask you to help me," Noah said.

On May 9, 2010, Barack Obama used his commencement address at Hampton University to take on the question of attention and attention deficit, of substance and spectacle, of the need to mine these territories for a deeper meaning, one defined by nuance and intellectual grace. Here's what he said to the graduates:

> Meanwhile, you're coming of age in a 24/7 media environment that bombards us with all kinds of content and exposes us to all kinds of arguments, some of which don't always rank that high on the truth meter. And with iPods and iPads; and Xboxes and PlayStations—none of which I know how to work—information becomes a distraction, a diversion, a form of entertainment, rather than a tool of empowerment, rather than the means of emancipation. So all of this is not only putting pressure on you; it's putting new pressure on our country and on our democracy.
>
> Class of 2010, this is a period of breathtaking change, like few others in our history. We can't stop these changes, but we can channel them, we can shape them, we can adapt to them. And education is what can allow us to do so. It can fortify you, as it did earlier generations, to meet the tests of your own time.

Almost immediately, Obama was derided across the internet for being out of touch. On Twitter, users referred to the speech as the "State of the iPad Address," while Gawker posted a response (called "Why Does Barack Obama Hate the iPad?"), in which contributor Max Read wondered, "Really . . . what is he even talking about here?" On the Huffington Post, an Associated Press story was illustrated with two photographs—of Obama and Apple chairman Steve Jobs juxtaposed to look like they were at odds. In a "Quick Poll" attached to the piece, 57.01 percent of respondents agreed with the president, although more telling may be the thirty-three hundred reactions on the comments thread. "Yes, Mr. Obama," read one such post, "what is wrong with a healthy discourse and the exchange of ideas and thoughts via the internet? FACTS getting in the way of your Socialist agenda??" Another warned, "You Obamozombies are falling for this red herring hook, line and sinker. What he was really doing was setting up the justification of regulating the Net"; while a third suggested that "Obama feels we should not have too much information, its [sic] bad for us. I am sure he and his team will come up with a fair way to limit and screen the information we recive [sic]. Thank God we have Him to control the information flow to us!"

On the one hand, this is in the nature of a comments thread, which, with its anonymous or pseudonymous posters, thrives on the noise of constant conversation, all the innuendo and cross-posting, the tiny feuds and insignificant disputes. On the other, it's emblematic of precisely the sort of degraded cultural conversation to which Obama refers. "We are in a shaky moment," David Denby writes in his jeremiad *Snark: It's Mean, It's Personal, and It's Ruining Our Conversation*, "a moment of transition, and I think it's reasonable to ask: What are we doing to ourselves?" A few pages later, Denby carries the argument to its logical conclusion: "The trouble with today's snarky pipsqueaks who break off a sentence or two, or who write a couple of mean paragraphs, is that they don't go far enough; they don't have a coherent view of life. Spinning around in the media from moment to moment, they don't stand for anything, push for anything; they're mere opportunists without dedication, and they don't win any victories."

What Denby is lamenting is the lack of a larger framework, the absence of any wider point of view. That's the problem with the culture of the comments thread, which, for all its pretense toward open conversation, adds up to little more than a collection of parallel monologues. In his 2004 book *Gag Rule*, Lewis Lapham brings us back to *Common Sense*, arguing that what Paine excelled at—and what we, as a society, appear to have lost—is the ability to carry out a logical argument. For Lapham, that's a consequence of the decline in reading and the rise of an electronic landscape in which everything has come to coexist in a never-ending present tense. "Nothing necessarily follows from anything else," he cautions. "Sequence becomes merely additive instead of causative—the images bereft of memory, speaking to their own reflections in a vocabulary better suited to the sale of a product than to the articulation of a thought." I'm not sure I agree with him completely; there is plenty of nuanced thinking on the internet, and plenty of books (*Mein Kampf, The Turner Diaries, The Protocols of the Elders of Zion*) that turn logical argument on its head. It's not the medium, in other words, but the message. And yet, Lapham is onto something when he refers to the breakdown of sequential thinking (*images bereft of memory, speaking to their own reflections*), the collapse of history, of context. "The Future was shown as empty highway," George W. S. Trow wrote thirty years ago in *Within the Context of No Context*, and from the vantage point of that future, it's stunning just how right he was.

Of course, I'm picking and choosing here, grabbing examples—from the internet, from my reading—that support my point of view. I'm stacking

the deck, manipulating the data, framing, always framing, an idea. Of the thirty-three hundred comments on
that Huffington Post piece about Obama, I've selected
three as a representative sample, but they're representative only of what I want them to be. Scroll down
the thread and you'll find plenty of intelligent and
cogent comments; you'll also find plenty that are far
more vitriolic, written in a patois barely approximat-
ing English, fulminating, outraged, like small embryos
of hate. And yet, representative or otherwise, what do
any of these reactions have to do with the thought that
set the thread in motion, the notion of the risks we face
when information becomes "a distraction, a diversion, a
form of entertainment, rather than a tool of empowerment, rather than the means of emancipation"? Where
is the engagement, the deeper reading, the sense of
what, exactly, is at stake?

If anything, all this endless back-and-forth is relevant only inasmuch as it illustrates Obama's point
by example, highlighting distraction and diversion in
action, masquerading as part of a public dialogue. This
is how we interact now, by mouthing off, steering every
conversation back to our agendas, skimming the surface
of each subject looking for an opportunity to spew. We
see it on blogs and in emails, on television talk shows,
in public meetings and community forums; we are a

culture that seems unable to concentrate, to pursue a line of thought or tolerate a conflicting point of view. Here's Fitzgerald again, from *The Crack-Up*: "The test of a first-rate intelligence is the ability to hold two opposed ideas in the mind at the same time, and still retain the ability to function." That was written in February 1936, at a moment not dissimilar to this one, fraught with economic and political instability, with the specter of conflict abroad and demagoguery at home. Hitler, Father Coughlin, Hirohito, Huey Long, Mussolini, the Great Depression, the show trials, the Dust Bowl, the Spanish Civil War: this is the context within which Fitzgerald wrote. Now compare that with the confrontation, during an August 18, 2009, town hall about health-care reform in Dartmouth, Massachusetts, between Congressman Barney Frank and a woman who asked how Frank could support Obama's "Nazi" policies. "You stand there," Frank replied, "with a picture of the president defaced to look like Hitler, and compare the effort to increase health care to the Nazis. My answer to you is, as I said before, it is a tribute to the First Amendment that this kind of vile, contemptible nonsense is so freely propagated." But it's his next remark ("Ma'am, trying to have a conversation with you would be like trying to argue with a dining room table. I have no interest in doing it.") that illustrates the depth of the divide. Frank is right, of course, but unspoken is a larger question: how do we even begin to bridge this kind of distance, logical or otherwise?

It's different with a book, or any long-form piece of writing; these are slower, deeper, *quieter*. As readers, we are asked to slip inside the text, and if we can't help but bring our personalities and perceptions to the process, the participation required leads to an inevitable empathy. Among the particular pleasures of reading, Jane Smiley suggests in *13 Ways of Looking at the Novel*, "was something outside of the authors' plot making and character drawing and theme organizing—it was the pleasure I gained from the authors' passing observations or remarks. I came to see these passing phrases as . . . precious artifacts of what a man—say, Walter Scott— happened to see one day while he was walking down a street in 1810; or what a woman, Elizabeth Bowen, happened to feel one evening while dancing the fox-trot in 1925; or what another man, Nikolai Gogol, happened to smell and hear by the banks of the Dnieper River one morning in 1820." Precious artifacts, indeed, although not merely of the past. Rather, what Smiley is tracing is the way time collapses in the act of reading—or both collapses and expands. Yes, to read Scott or Bowen or Gogol is to experience firsthand a moment that might otherwise be lost to us, but even more, it is to be brought in touch with our commonality as human beings. The struggles are the same, the frailties and excitations, the vulnerabilities, the petty jealousies, the desires. Saint Augustine may have composed his *Confessions* sixteen hundred years ago, but when he details his spiritual upheaval, his attempts to find meaning in the face of transient existence, the immediacy of his longing obliterates the temporal divide. "To hold all of these moments in my mind," Smiley writes, "to have access to them, is to have a broad sense of the world." As to why this is important *in the present*, she explains:

> In a world where weapons of mass destruction
> are permanent features of the landscape, I
> cannot help believing that a lively sense of
> the reality of other consciousnesses on the
> part of those whose fingers are on the trigger
> is essential to human survival. The novel
> has made a world in which people are fairly
> adept at both feeling and thinking, and at
> thinking about feeling. The way in which
> novels are created—someone is seized by
> inspiration and then works out his inspiration
> methodically by writing, observing, writing,

observing, thinking through, and writing again—is by nature deliberate, dominated neither by reason nor emotion. Perched on the cusp between the particular and the general, between expertise and common sense, the novel promotes compromise, and especially promotes the idea that lessons can be learned, if not by the characters, then by the author and the reader. The world of the novel is a rational world; even while the author and the characters are lamenting its irrationality, cause-and-effect relationships can be teased out of events and recognized, if only after the fact.

Smiley may be writing about the novel, but what she's getting at is something all books share: their sense of flow, their *linearity*, a condition that defines even the least linear works. Although *Cain's Book* bills itself as an antinovel, it ends up offering, despite Trocchi's best efforts to eclipse our expectations, its own odd kind of story, or a series of overlapping stories, tracing the author's sensibility (or that of his fictional alter ego) in fits and starts. In *Tristram Shandy*, Laurence Sterne gives us a masterpiece of digression, yet he still must build the novel around its central character's life. Even James Joyce's *Finnegans Wake*, perhaps the most famous, if unread—and yes, I'll admit, I haven't read it, not in its entirety, not even close, although I've done my share of dipping in and out of it, like a man on the beach tentatively touching his toes to the edge of a sprawling sea—nonlinear work in English literature, operates from the basic structural premise of the dream-narrative, where inference and association trump logic; it is a feedback loop, a Möbius strip, in which the last and first lines, unfinished fragments, link up to frame the never-ending cycle of the book. "A way a lone a last a loved a long the / riverrun, past Eva and Adam's, from swerve of shore to bend of bay, brings us by a commodius vicus of recirculation back to Howth Castle and Environs," this backwards sentence reads, and although it probably defeats the purpose of the novel to reconstruct it in that way, it also offers a beautiful reminder that even the most apparently formless efforts come with shapes and contexts (*a commodius vicus of recirculation*) of their own.

At the heart of all this is the issue of time, which Joyce understood. "History, Stephen said, is a nightmare from which I am trying to awake," he writes early in *Ulysses*, and it's a line that resonates. Who hasn't felt that sense of being trapped, of being caught against your will between the relentless forward motion of the present and the inescapable fixedness of the past? When I first read Joyce, as a college senior in a graduate *Ulysses* seminar, that sentence seemed a cry in the dark, akin to Dylan Thomas's "Rage, rage against the dying of the light." Here was Stephen Dedalus, a young man in his twenties, lamenting the existential condition, that we are condemned to live and die with no say over the matter; "born, never asked," as Laurie Anderson once sang. Later, I began to see this in a broader way, as less dirge than observation—bitter, yes, but touched in equal measure with an unconscious breath of resignation, the recognition that it was not just biology or metaphysics that stood stacked against us, but indeed time itself, not as a philosophical abstraction but as a concrete and relentless force.

"One must believe in the reality of Time," Simone Weil wrote in her *Notebooks*. "Otherwise one is just dreaming." It's fascinating that, in her choice of time as a metaphor, she unconsciously echoes *Ulysses* and *Finnegans Wake*. Joyce and Weil were contemporaries, after a fashion. Both died in the early 1940s, just before the bomb rendered our traditional conceptions of history forever obsolete. And yet, if their sense of time seems in some way oppositional—one seeking to refute it and the other to accept it—I can't help but see a bit of common ground between them, a recognition that time is all we have. This is the point, that we live in time, that we understand ourselves in relation to its passage. It may be the thing that will ultimately devour us, but without it we lose a sense of who we are.

Time, however, is the enemy in contemporary culture, less a source of context than constraint. We bridle against its limitations—not existentially but in far more prosaic terms—subdividing it into the merest bits and pieces, translating it into dollars gained or lost. "Take, for instance, these clients of ours who provide [directory assistance] service in Manhattan," explains the main character of Assaf Gavron's novel *Almost Dead*, an Israeli who works for a company that helps streamline corporate operations. "They've got a couple of thousand operators in New York answering calls coming in non-stop— 5.5 million phone calls a day in search of telephone numbers. If we can save one second from each call we save 5.5 million seconds a day, which is 63 days, or almost three working months of an employee." The book is a black comedy (about suicide bombing, of all things), but this part of it, anyway, is no exaggeration; it's a snapshot of the way we live. Most of us carry hand-held devices more powerful than the most versatile computers of a decade ago, yet rather than liberating us, they shave seconds off our downtime, as if it were something to be maximized. We check email, Facebook, Twitter, work and leisure websites as a matter of reflex: in restaurants, with our families, in the car.

Sometimes, of course, this can be useful. Recently, while out to dinner, a friend told Rae and me about a Geoff Dyer lecture at the Getty Center in Los Angeles called "How Do We Experience Art?" Dyer's argument, our friend explained, was that we immerse in art as (wait for it) a narrative, that it unfolds not as a fixed encounter but rather as something that gets inside us in a more sequential way. To illustrate the point, Dyer invoked Walter De Maria's *The Lightning Field*, a land art installation built in 1977 in western New Mexico, consisting of four hundred stainless-steel poles arranged in a rectangular grid. The motivation for *The Lightning Field* is not unlike that of any work of narrative; we are meant to experience it in time. To make sure of this, visitors are required to stay over at the site, spending the night in a small cabin on the grounds.

As it happens, I had read about *The Lightning Field* in Erin Hogan's *Spiral Jetta: A Road Trip through the Land Art of the American West*. Hogan admits that she was underwhelmed at first by De Maria's installation, until at dawn, she had the transformative experience she'd sought. "I was conscious only of the crunch of my footsteps," she writes, recalling a morning walk through the field. "It was not just the individual poles or neighborhoods that were unveiled; it was the sense of choice and possibility. Vistas opened up, new views appeared with every footstep and ray of light." Although I love the idea of a work of art that changes depending on how you move within it, love its promise of interaction, agency, I had never thought about *The Lightning Field* as a narrative until our friend began to recount the Dyer lecture. Now I could see the lines, the stories, inherent in its landscape, the way time became not just a métier but a motif, an element of the work. As our friend talked, I took out my BlackBerry and opened the browser, looking for photographs of the site. Rae didn't know *The Lightning Field,* so when I found a picture of the poles at sunset, silhouetted against a sky shot through with red and gold, I passed it to her. The image was small, no bigger than a postage stamp, the poles as thin as filaments or wires. It took a minute to make out, like one of those optical illusion drawings— or, perhaps, like *The Lightning Field* itself. Rae looked at the small screen, her eyes reflecting its glow as the picture coalesced. I could see a glint of something, rec-ognition or excitement or anticipation. "We need to go there," she said.

Here, we have an example of how technology can enlarge us, can offer access to things we didn't even know we didn't know. Here, we have an example of the intrusion that works, that adds up to something bigger, that illuminates an experience, that gives it meaning, gives it depth. And yet, for me at least, this is the exception, as our oversaturated culture collapses into an ever-present now. Far more common is a sense of skittering across the surface, a feeling of drift, both mental and emotional, in which time and context become unmoored. This is the nature of my distraction: the world is always too close at hand. I can check my email in an instant, and twenty, thirty times a day, I do. What am I looking for? Something, every thing, a way of staying on top of the information . . . it doesn't matter. The looking is an end unto itself. I Google myself, or read the Google Alerts that pop up in my inbox, links leading me to reprints of my pieces in regional papers, blog posts critiquing me and/or my work. It all seems so important in the moment, and yet none of it sticks. Meanwhile, I can tap into whatever momentary obsession gnaws at me—Obama's poll numbers, the reopening of the Etan Patz case, the state of the New York Yankees' bullpen—and read not one article about it but a dozen, watching video, looking at photographs, recycling the same information, the same quotes and figures, in different configurations, parsing and reparsing as if it might yield something new.

That the conversation rarely changes is not a problem; rather, it is entirely the point. I don't want to be challenged but to be soothed.

It's a key distinction, although often overlooked: that in a world of endless information (hyperconnectivity, the 24/7 news stream, call it what you will), we face endless anxiety about our ability to keep up, to maintain a place amid the onslaught, to make sense of all the data and what it means. Traditionally, that was the role of the gatekeepers, the arbiters, but their brand of top-down authority has fallen out of favor in our flattened age. I don't lament their passing, not exactly, since they kept a lot of voices out of the dialogue. Yet I'm also wary of any cultural revolution that denies the importance of expertise, that turns away from experience, that seeks, like China in the 1960s, to create everything anew. (*Information becomes a distraction, a diversion, a form of entertainment, rather than a tool of empowerment, rather than the means of emancipation.*) That's the revolutionary fallacy, the fallacy of all "Year One" thinking, from the Bastille to *Never Mind the Bollocks*. There is no Year One, there is no outside, there is no breaking point at which we shed the past, either personal or public, and take the Great Leap Forward into a newer world.

And yet, we live now in a culture where the Great Leap Forward happens every minute, where time and context have grown so condensed that even anxiety doesn't hit us fast enough. How do we pause when we must know everything in an instant? How do we ruminate when we are constantly expected to respond? How do we immerse in something (an idea, an emotion, a decision) when we are no longer willing to give ourselves the space to reflect? Think about the speed of the news cycle. We want information reported, digested, and analyzed—at times before the story has finished playing out. This is not a critique of technology, although technology has surely kicked it into overdrive. Instead, this has to do with how we think about our culture, how we think about our history itself.

Among the most discussed books of early 2010 were two works of biographical reportage: David Remnick's *The Bridge: The Life and Rise of Barack Obama* and Jonathan Alter's *The Promise: President Obama, Year One.* Remnick ended his book with Obama's election to the presidency, while Alter covered the first twelve months of the administration, adding new material just before publication to stay up-to-date on health-care reform. On the one hand, both projects are testaments to technology, the technology by which a book can come to market quickly, can approach the imprimatur of instant news. On the other, they speak to a larger dislocation, our desire to interpret things even as we're living through them, to know everything about the world we occupy *now*. How can we possibly assess Obama's presidency when his first term is not halfway done? Where do we make room for uncertainty, for acknowledging that there is much we don't understand? In December 2009, a study by the Global Information Industry Center at the University of California, San Diego, found that, "in 2008, Americans consumed information for about 1.3 trillion hours, an average of almost 12 hours per day. Consumption totaled 3.6 zettabytes and 10,845 trillion words, corresponding to 100,500 words and 34 giga-bytes for an average person on an average day." One hundred thousand words is the equivalent of a three-hundred-page novel, and it's encouraging to learn that we all read this much. Still, given the fragmentation, the back-and-forth between texting, email, print, Twitter, blogs and other websites—not to mention audio and video—what is the GIIC really tracking? Not our interaction with the word so much as the logistics of a collective data dump.

This is where reading, real reading, comes in— because it demands space, because by drawing us back from the primacy of the instant it restores time to us in a more fundamental way. It's not possible to read a book in the present, for books exist in many moments all at once. There is the immediate experience of reading, but also the chronology of the narrative, as well as of the characters and author, all of whom bear their own relationships to time. There is the fixity of the text, which doesn't change whether it was written yesterday or a thousand years ago. Perhaps most important, there is the way reading requires us to pay attention, which cannot help but return us to the realm of inner life. "My experience is what I agree to attend to," William James noted in his 1905 treatise *Psychology.* "Only those items which I notice shape my mind—without selective interest, experience is an utter chaos." The GIIC report suggests how far we may have strayed. In a piece for the *Times of London*, Richard Woods and Chris Hastings quote Roger Bohn, a coauthor of the study: "I think one thing is clear: our attention is being chopped into shorter intervals and that is probably not good for thinking deeper thoughts." They also talk to Edward Hallowell, a psychiatrist working with attention deficit disorder. "Never before in human history," he claims, "have our brains had to process as much information as they do today. We have a generation of people who . . . are so busy processing information from all directions they are losing the tendency to think and to feel. [And] much of what they are exposed to is superficial. People are sacrificing depth and feeling and becoming cut off and disconnected from other people."

This, of course, is the classic knock on technology, that in the name of connectivity it distances us from each other and, even more, from ourselves. Our constant impulse to tweet, to text, to post status updates offers the illusion of intimacy by allowing us to share the most mundane details of existence ("I think I'll reheat the stir-fry for lunch") without revealing anything much of substance at all. Again, I'm not sure I agree with this assessment completely, although it's impossible not to agree with it in part. I have Facebook friends I've never met, which only degrades the notion of what *friend* means, and whenever I go on the site (less and less these days, for this very reason), I spend time reading their updates or deciding not to read them, depending on my state of mind. And yet, I've also made, or remade, real connections via Facebook. Last year, during a visit to San Francisco, I went out for drinks with two old high school friends I hadn't seen in thirty years. That was a stretch for me, since I am not, by nature, nostalgic. Still, although I was curious enough to find out what these people were doing, I have not been curious enough to look them up again.

All of this suggests a complicated conundrum, between what we once were and what we are in the process of becoming. Such a conundrum is both personal and collective, having to do, on the one hand, with the way that in the floating world of cyberspace nothing is ever truly past or lost and, on the other, with the unintended consequences of this instant access, how it alters identity and memory. These issues, of course, have informed the human experience ever since there was a human experience. "The past is never dead," William Faulkner wrote in *Requiem for a Nun.* "It's not even past." For Faulkner, however, the word *past* meant something specific (if also elusive): the weight of history, of heritage, beneath which the best we have to hope for is "the temporary abeyance of . . . despair and the isolation of that doom [we] could not escape." In *The Sound and the Fury,* that great harmonic convergence of a novel, Quentin Compson—schizophrenic, on the verge of suicide—puts it in the starkest possible terms. "I give you the mausoleum of all hope and desire," he recalls his father saying, after presenting Quentin with a watch, a family heirloom. "I give it to you not that you may remember time, but that you might forget it now and then for a moment and not spend all your breath trying to conquer it. Because no battle is ever won he said. They are not even fought. The field only reveals to man his own folly and despair, and victory is an illusion of philosophers and fools." As usual, Faulkner is writing on a couple of levels, the metaphysical (*One must believe in the reality of Time. Otherwise one is just dreaming.*) and the personal. Even when we seek to forget it, he means to tell us, we exist at the mercy of the past.

And yet, what does the past mean now that it can expose itself at the touch of a button, now that the debris of personal history exists at not just *our* fingertips but also those of anyone with access to our electronic profiles? In a 2009 essay in the *Los Angeles Times* (a piece that, full disclosure, I commissioned and edited), Rich Cohen considers the coming-of-age novel in the era of social networking and wonders whether it will soon be obsolete. "To write about kids from, say, Central School, Glencoe, Ill., circa 1982," he suggests, "you need the illusion that you have left that party and gone on to another, better party, where you can trash your old friends without fear of consequence. They can't hear you, can't reach you, don't even know where you are. I mean, when you write such a book, what are you doing if not talking behind the back of an entire town?" But there's more at stake here than the fate of a literary genre, as Cohen makes clear in his concluding paragraphs:

Facebook, with its flow of useless particularity, makes it impossible to forget, thus impossible to remember. Memory is really the story left behind by forgetting—the essence that remains when the years have stripped away all that useless particularity. You remember as much by forgetting as you do by remembering. But on Facebook, the past becomes the wound that is never allowed to heal so never scars into deep experience.

The Buddhists say do not describe the water until the mud has settled and you can see its true essence, but the mud never does settle online. The water is continually stirred up, making remembering impossible. The memory in your mind is replaced by a detail posted on a Web page, which may be more accurate but is probably less true. Gone is the friend you knew from home. Gone is the sled and the lake and the winter. Gone are the stories that existed in the gap between imagining and knowing and, with them, the distance that turned the particular into the universal and the mundane into the romantic.

In this way, the past, seeming to get closer, actually gets further away.

Impossible to forget, thus impossible to remember.
There it is, the point precisely, the place where memory,
technology, and the self intersect. "We have to remember
to stop because we have to stop to remember," Judith
Shulevitz writes in *The Sabbath World: Glimpses of
a Different Order of Time.* For Shulevitz, this is the
appeal of the Sabbath—whether orthodox or unortho-
dox, whether as part of a spiritual tradition or recast
as a strategy to reconnect. Late in the book, she refers
to David Levy, "a professor at the Information School
at University of Washington," who has begun to work
toward what he calls "informational environmental-
ism," in which, "just as we fight to save marshlands and
old-growth forests from development and pollution, . . .
so we need to fight to save ourselves from the 'pollut-
ants' of communications overload: the overabundance
of information that turns us into triagers and manag-
ers, rather than readers; the proliferation of bad or useless or ersatz information; the forces that push us to
process quickly rather than thoughtfully." If we ignore
such an imperative, "we risk becoming cut off from the
world, rather than more connected; less able to make
wise decisions, rather than better informed; and, in
the end, less human." The solution? "To cultivate unhur-
ried activities and quiet places, sanctuaries in time and
space for reflection and contemplation." A technological

Sabbath, in other words. In March 2010, an organization called Sabbath Manifesto proposed exactly that, launching a website (the irony, the irony) and articulating ten principles "open for your unique interpretation . . . as we carve a weekly timeout into our lives." Here's the list:

01. Avoid technology.

02. Connect with loved ones.

03. Nurture your health.

04. Get outside.

05. Avoid commerce.

06. Light candles.

07. Drink wine.

08. Eat bread.

09. Find silence.

10. Give back.

There's not a lot here with which to argue; for the most part, it's all common sense. Who wouldn't want to "connect with loved ones"? Or drink wine, eat bread, and light candles while nurturing our health? At the same time, the idea that we have to give ourselves these sorts of conscious reminders tells us something about the culture in which we live. "Cell-phone and text-messaging and social-networking technologies have begun to wash away at adamantine 'mechanical time,' the unyielding time of clocks," Shulevitz writes, "and to suspend us within 'mobile time,' which can be made to flow whichever way we want." For her, this is primarily a practical dynamic, in which technology allows us to bend time to our needs rather than the other way around. But what about the philosophical considerations, the effect of mobile time not only on how we function but also on how we see the world? "Speed becomes its own self-justifying value," Eva Hoffman argues in her 2009 meditation *Time*. "It fragments time internally, as well as externally; for without some sense that disparate occurrences are linked through coherent meanings or aims, there is no way to connect the moments in which they occur." What's more, it is technology's efficiency—its ability to store vast amounts of information and to make it accessible immediately—that may also be its biggest risk. "To try to grasp paradigmatic change as it happens," Hoffman acknowledges, "is perhaps to wander where angels fear to tread." That doesn't stop her, though, from offering a few general observations:

> On one level we are relegating more and more of our mental operations to various technologies, with digital devices increasingly acting

as prostheses for our faculties. We entrust
our sense of spatial orientation to satellite
navigation systems; we give mathematical
calculations over to the appropriate gadgets.
Indeed, the temptation is to let the computer
do much of the thinking for us. We can cut
and paste fragments from the internet and
hope that the collage adds up to something
coherent, or interestingly disjunctive.
Certainly, we have less need to remember
information ourselves when so much can
be stored in our computer's memory. The
feats of memory recorded in oral cultures, or
performed by Soviet poets and writers under
censorship, seem hardly credible within our
zeitgeist. Nadezhda Mandelstam memorized
all of her husband's poetry because it was
too hazardous to write it down. Solzhenitsyn
committed to memory each page he wrote
when he was imprisoned in the Gulag, and
then destroyed the evidence. Such powers of
retention are unimaginable to most of us and
they may become even more so, as we transfer
memory to the many storage places available
to us—there to be filed away, for instant and
effortless retrieval.

> By transposing aspects of thought and
> memory to technology we are externalizing
> our mental operations. But both the mind and
> the psyche require internality.

What Hoffman is talking about is identity, which we build out of the shard ends of experience and memory. This is the raw subjective stuff of living, and here, too, technology provokes an existential question about how we relate to history, individual or otherwise. I'm not referring, necessarily, to Mandelstam or Solzhenitsyn, although it's in our interest to keep their stories close at hand. But even on the most mundane terms, electronic memory strips a certain agency from our relationship with the past. Here's an example: When I was seven, my father took me to my first baseball game. It was September 20, 1968, a Friday night, Yankees versus Red Sox at the old Yankee Stadium. I know all this because I remember it, just as I remember much about the evening with a clarity bordering on the hallucinogenic. I remember that we sat in the loge on the first-base side, and that as we came up out of the ramp, the field shone in sharp contrasts, deep green and red brown, when I saw it beneath the floodlights for the first time. I remember that Mickey Mantle hit a home run—the final major-league home

run of his career—and that Carl Yastrzemski hom-
ered for Boston, and that the pitching matchup was
Fritz Peterson against Jim Lonborg, and that the Red
Sox won four to three. After forty-two years, these are
insignificant details, the fragments of a meaningless
game played late in an undistinguished season. And
yet, to me, they are something more than that: a starting point, a creation myth, the moment that my fascination with baseball, and with the Yankees, could be
said to have truly taken shape.

This is the way memory resonates, the way it works
within us, framing our experiences and giving them
coherent form. It's a matter of engagement, of being
present; I recall that game so clearly because I paid
attention to it as I had never paid attention to anything
in my life. I've never seen a clip from it on YouTube, not
even of the Mantle homer. There is nothing, no visual
evidence, only the acuity of the images as they exist
within my brain. These images are so vivid that, at one
point, I began to doubt them, since recollection usually
doesn't remain so clear. When I was in college, I looked
up the game on microfilm (it happened almost entirely
as I remembered, except that I had always thought a
third home run, by Yankees' right fielder Bill Robinson,
had been an inside-the-park job, which the record con-
tradicts); and a few years ago, I bookmarked a summary

on my browser, which allows me instant access not just to the line and box scores but also to a variety of statistical breakdowns, including one that dissects the action play-by-play.

On the one hand, this is nothing if not a metaphor for information overload, since who needs such detail at close hand? Does it enhance my life in any way to know that Mantle's home run came in the bottom of the third with two outs, or that the next batter, Roy White, ended the inning by flying out to left? No, it only fuels a fascination with facts over imagination, a sense of experience as somehow quantifiable, in which memory can be pinned down and verified and the surface of a situation is more important than what happens underneath. What those statistics don't (*can't*) encompass is what it felt like to be there—not to the world at large, but to me. They cannot contain the intangibles, the individual experience, what it meant to sit beside my father as he explained the game. This is the origin of narrative, the moment when we internalize the external, when we begin to alchemize it into something uniquely ours. Yet how do we make room for narrative now that we can post or save *everything*—phone numbers, photos, videos, our most personal opinions—which alleviates us of the responsibility to remember any of it for ourselves? What about selectivity? (*Without selective interest, experience is an utter chaos.*) And what do we make of the fact that all this information, all these tags and posts and comments, this flotsam from a culture awash in distraction, remain part of the floating, time-less present of the cyberverse, meaning we can never get away from who we were?

Here, I think, we see the roots of the false sense of certainty, of rectitude, that has come to dominate almost every corner of our chaotic public life. Just look at the reaction to another baseball game, the imper-fect one thrown by Detroit Tigers pitcher Armando Galarraga against the Cleveland Indians on June 2, 2010. Galarraga was one out away from the twenty-first perfect game ever pitched when an umpire named Jim Joyce (proof, perhaps, that Einstein was wrong when he said, "God does not play dice") blew a routine play at first base, calling Cleveland batter Jason Donald safe when he was clearly out. In that instant, the mistake became a fact, and the perfect game became the most famous one-hitter in the history of the sport. Baseball has always been enlarged by just such moments, the weird and the wonderful, the games that don't quite fit. Think of Harvey Haddix, who, on May 26, 1959, threw twelve perfect innings for the Pittsburgh Pirates against the Milwaukee Braves, only to lose the no-hitter, and the game, in the thirteenth. Or Ernie Shore, a pitcher for the Boston Red Sox, who retired twenty-six consecutive batters on June 23, 1917, against the Washington Senators after relieving Babe Ruth, who walked the first batter and was thrown out of the game.

These are not events so much as they are stories, threads in the fabric of baseball's narrative, much as Galarraga's is. Still, in the aftermath of Joyce's blown call, there were death threats and an outcry to overturn the play. Even the White House weighed in, after a fashion: "I hope that baseball awards a perfect game to that pitcher," press secretary Robert Gibbs declared. Everywhere you looked, there was that video: Galarraga covering first base, taking the throw from Miguel Cabrera, Joyce's arms stretched wide in the safe call (*history . . . is a nightmare from which I am trying to awake*). It's a compelling bit of footage, Detroit's Comerica Park falling suddenly silent, Galarraga's teammates staring from the dugout, and the pitcher himself, the trace of a grin flickering across his face like a rumor, as if he can't believe what he's just seen. Yet rather than embrace the moment—and what a moment: a once-in-a-lifetime situation, a narrative that has literally *never before been told*—we fixate on how, or whether, to correct it, ignoring serendipity, human error, the glorious intercession of the unanticipated, in favor of the high-definition clarity (read: morality) of the digital replay screen.

Such a reaction is indicative of how we often miss the forest for the trees. If we frame every situation in terms of right and wrong, we never have to wrestle with complexity; if we define the world in narrow bands of black and white, we don't have to parse out endless shades of gray. This emerges in our relationship with reading also . . . in our relationship with reading, maybe, most of all. Books, after all, have long been a source of consternation in the culture, both from those who love them and from those who don't. Back when I was an adolescent, reading my way through family gatherings with a fierceness born of isolation, my grandmother used to bother me to put the book down, to stop isolating myself. It's no small irony to hear the same arguments used now against the computer, although, of course, the page and the screen are different frames. Still, just how different remains to be seen, in a landscape defined increasingly by e-reading, where the conversation has shifted fundamentally toward technology.

E-books may not yet occupy a huge corner of the market (5 percent of total U.S. book sales in the first quarter of 2010, notes a Book Industry Study Group report released in late May 2010, up from 1.5 percent in 2009), but they are one of the few growth areas in an industry widely regarded as moribund. According to the Association of American Publishers, e-book purchases jumped 176.6 percent between 2008 and 2009 and another 252 percent (*252 percent?*) in the first quarter of 2010. Even keeping in mind that the numbers are nebulous—"From consumer demand, to devices and DRM schemes, to piracy concerns and reliable sales data," writes Guy LeCharles Gonzalez in a June 9, 2010, piece for *Digital Book World*, "the nascent but undeniably booming e-book market is becoming a smoke and mirrored mess for anyone looking for straight answers"— there's no question that these developments affect how we read. In its 2009 study *Reading on the Rise*, which concluded that "literary reading," defined as that involving "novels and short stories, plays, or poems," had risen 3.5 percent in the years between 2002 and 2008, the National Endowment for the Arts considered online reading habits for the first time. You can think about this data through a variety of filters, as significant cultural indicator or statistical anomaly, but either way, they suggest a landscape in which our relationship with books and writing has grown increasingly complex.

I first noticed such a shift in my own reading in late 2007, when I read Zachary Lazar's novel *Sway*, which interweaves three iconic stories (the rise of the Rolling Stones from 1962 through Altamont; the long, strange trip of underground filmmaker Kenneth Anger; and the saga of Charles Manson associate and convicted murderer Bobby Beausoleil) to get at the dark side of the 1960s, the moment when the Age of Aquarius imploded into Luciferian light. *Sway* is an odd book, all glittery surfaces and collapsing possibilities—yet the strangest thing about it may be that which has the least to do with the language on the page. Instead, it's the role of history, of documentary evidence, the bizarre double vision that accompanies a novel for which so much source material exists as external counternarrative. Reading *Sway*, I couldn't stay away from the internet, looking up Anger's 1947 short *Fireworks* on YouTube after finishing Lazar's account of it, then doing the same with *Scorpio Rising*, the 1964 biker film that made its creator a minor celebrity when it was banned in California. As for the Stones, I kept playing and replaying footage from *Gimme Shelter*: Meredith Hunter stabbed to death by the Hell's Angels during "Sympathy for the Devil," as if the song truly were an invocation, as if it had unleashed a force the band could not control.

This is one of the driving ideas behind both Lazar's book and the Maysles brothers' documentary, which seek to make us look beneath the surface by framing the Dionysian rituals of the 1960s through a darker lens.

As such, it seemed only natural that I should *see* it, that I should put down the book and engage with the era's contradictions on the most direct terms. Still, each time I did, I found myself confronting another contradiction, between word and image, between what, for want of a better phrase, let's call interior and exterior life. Here we have the most essential distinction between books and pictures, moving or otherwise—the way the former gets at the outside from the inside, while for the latter it's the other way around. Language is internal; it asks us to create *our* images, *our* movies, *our* realities from someone else's words. This is the source of its power, that it is interactive in the truest sense. And yet, what do we do in a culture where we are constantly invited to step out of the frame, to externalize imagination, to rethink how the process works? Each time I put down *Sway*, I had to ask myself this question, had to wonder whether I was getting the point (triangulating the material, becoming more of an active participant, meeting Lazar somewhere in the middle) or missing it entirely, removing myself from the text in favor of events. I felt torn—as if I were enhancing the novel and diminishing it at once. It's not the only time I've read a book this way. Thurston Clarke's *The Last Campaign: Robert F. Kennedy and 82 Days That Inspired America* sent me to YouTube to watch hours of video chronicling

RFK's tragic 1968 presidential run. *Sway*, though, is not a work of history; it is a novel with historical undertones. And in the end, my strategy for engaging it only leaves me with another set of questions. Such as: Does it enhance or diffuse the power of the novel to read it in conjunction with the computer, to look up and literally watch the scenes take place? And: What does this mean for memory, for reading, for our own ability to invoke, and then evoke, a shared narrative dream?

These are not just academic questions, but rather ones that get to the heart of how we interact with narrative in an information-saturated world. "Over the last few years," Nicholas Carr writes in *The Shallows: What the Internet Is Doing to Our Brains*, "I've had an uncomfortable sense that someone, or something, has been tinkering with my brain, remapping the neural circuitry, reprogramming the memory. My mind isn't going—so far as I can tell—but it's changing. I'm not thinking the way I used to think." For Carr, the issue is not so much intellectual, or social, as it is chemical: technology is rewiring the neurology of our brains. There's nothing new about such a process. "As long ago as 8000 B.C.," Carr notes, "people were using small clay tokens engraved with simple symbols to keep track of livestock and other goods. Interpreting even such rudimentary markings required the development of extensive new neural pathways in people's brains, connecting the visual cortex with nearby sense-making areas of the brain. Modern studies show that the neural activity along these pathways doubles or triples when we look at meaningful symbols as opposed to meaningless doodles." The paradox, of course, is that as our brain chemistry changes, we do also, until the issue of what it means to be human is, in its own way, up for grabs. Take reading, for instance, which Carr discusses at length . . . especially silent reading, which most of us take for granted as a condition of our daily lives. And yet, silent reading is learned behavior, requiring a force of will, of sustained concentration, that, in a very real sense, runs counter to what instinct would suggest. Carr explains:

> The natural state of the human brain, like that
> of the brains of most of our relatives in the
> animal kingdom, is one of distractedness. Our
> predisposition is to shift our gaze, and hence
> our attention, from one object to another,
> to be aware of as much of what's going on
> around us as possible. . . . Our fast-paced,
> reflexive shifts in focus were once crucial to
> our survival. They reduced the odds that a

predator would take us by surprise or that we'd overlook a nearby source of food. . . .

To read a book was to practice an unnatural process of thought, one that demanded sustained, unbroken attention to a single static object. It required readers to place themselves at what T. S. Eliot, in *Four Quartets*, would call "the still point of the turning world."

You can consider such a passage in a few different ways: as an expression of the relationship between civilization and abstraction, or even as a statement of the dangers of intellectual life. There's a reason, after all, that Plato made his case against poets in *The Republic*, although Carr argues that this is more an attack on the oral tradition than a dismissal of reading and writing per se. Regardless, the passage hints at a process not unlike evolution, a strategy for adapting to the circumstances in which we find ourselves. In the industrialized West, it's been a long time since most people had to worry about predators or the basic requirements for survival on any regular basis; we can assert ourselves in other ways. And if reading is not exactly active, it is assertive, connective even, in the most essential sense. According to a recent study undertaken by the Dynamic

Cognition Laboratory at Washington University and cited by Carr, fiction readers "mentally simulate each new situation encountered in a narrative. Details about actions and sensations are captured from the text and integrated with personal knowledge from past experiences." Even more, Carr continues, "the brain regions that are activated 'closely mirror those involved when people perform, imagine, or observe similar real-world activities.' Deep reading, says the study's lead researcher, Nicole Speer, 'is by no means a passive exercise.' The reader becomes the book."

The reader becomes the book. This is an important—perhaps the most important—point. What it suggests is that reading is a way to map, or imprint, certain emotional states or experiences, that it is a template by which we come to a reckoning with life. Such a reckoning can play out as a kind of interior rehearsal, or it can take shape in the transference we feel when we read a scene, any scene, that moves us, that allows us to empathize with the action or the characters. Reading is a form of self-identification that works, paradoxically, by encouraging us to identify with others, an abstract process that changes us in the most concrete of ways. Again, Jane Smiley, from *13 Ways of Looking at the Novel*:

When we talk about the death of the novel, what we are really talking about is the possibility that empathy, however minimal, would no longer be attainable by those for whom the novel has died. If the novel has died for the bureaucrats who run our country, then they are more likely not to pause before engaging in arrogant, narcissistic, and foolish policies. If the novel has died for men (and some publishers and critics say that men read fewer novels than they used to), then the inner lives of their friends and family members are a degree more closed to them than before. If the novel dies, or never lives, for children and teenagers who spend their time watching TV or playing video games, then they will always be somewhat mystified by others, and by themselves as well. If the novel should die, what is to replace it?

My guess is that mere technology will not kill the novel. It is too different from movies and other forms of visual entertainment to be replaced by them, nor do I believe that novels are bannable. Too many of them reside in private hands: they would be as hard to get rid of as guns and bullets. But novels can be

sidelined—dismissed to the seraglio, where
they are read by women and children and
have no effect on those in power. When that
happens, our society will be brutalized and
coarsened by people who speak rather like us
and look rather like us but who have no way of
understanding us or each other.

And yet, we may ultimately have no control over
what happens, over how we continue to evolve. Already,
barely two decades into the internet era, our brains
have reconfigured, reverting to a kind of informational
hunter-gatherer mode. "As [Marshall] McLuhan suggested," Carr writes, "media aren't just channels of
information. They supply the stuff of thought, but they
also shape the process of thought." And it happens fast.
In *The Shallows*, Carr describes a 2008 experiment,
conducted by UCLA's Memory and Aging Center, on
"the physiological and neurological effects of the use
of digital media." The findings are stunning, for what
they say about both the scope of these developments
and their speed. Scanning the brain function of twenty-
four volunteers—"a dozen experienced Web surfers,"
Carr tells us, "and a dozen novices"—as they did routine
Google searches, researchers found that "the computer-
savvy subjects used a specific network in the left front

part of the brain, known as the dorsolateral prefrontal cortex, [while] the internet-naïve subjects showed minimal, if any, activity in this area." After five days, in which the latter group was asked to spend an hour a day on the web, the volunteers were scanned again. "The exact same neural circuitry in the front part of the brain became active in the internet-naïve subjects," Carr notes, quoting the Memory and Aging Center report. "Five hours on the internet, and the naïve subjects had already rewired their brains." He goes on to cite other studies that track distinctions between reading and web surfing, concluding that because the computer requires us to use more parts of the brain than books do, it may actually (another paradox) help us keep our minds more acutely engaged. Still, it's a different kind of brain function, one that short-circuits concentration in favor of a kind of intellectual and emotional hit and run. "Whenever we, as readers, come upon a link," Carr observes, "we have to pause, for at least a split second, to allow our prefrontal cortex to evaluate whether or not we should click on it. The redirection of our mental resources, from reading words to making judgments, may be imperceptible to us—our brains are quick—but it's been shown to impede comprehension and retention, particularly when it's repeated frequently."

All of this raises yet another question: that of whether what we do on the computer should even be classified as reading or if it is, in fact, something else. The same might be asked about my experience of *Sway* or *The Last Campaign*—a hybrid process involving the best (or worst) of both worlds. Perhaps the most useful way to look at this is through the filter of "secondary orality," a concept framed by Walter Ong in his 1982 book *Orality and Literacy: The Technologizing of the Word*. Ong's idea is that, in an era of nearly instantaneous, and collaborative, mass communication, the linearity of print or written language elides into a more fluid stew of information that mirrors the back-and-forth of oral cultures even as it relies on the most highly developed technologies. If that seems like one more paradox . . . well, this is where we are. "Writing and print and the computer," Carr quotes Ong, "are all ways of technologizing the word," and it's a statement worth remembering, if only because it reminds us that books, too, are part of the technological continuum. It's been less than six hundred years, remember, since Gutenberg sparked the original information revolution, in a moment not unlike the one we are currently living through. That revolution, too, had its detractors, including the fifteenth-century Venetian judge Filippo di Strata, who declared flatly, "The pen is a virgin; the printing press, a whore."

And yet, even someone like di Strata might have been hard-pressed to sum up the challenges of the present in equally definitive terms. For that, we need a different metaphor. In 2007, shortly after the release of his novel *The Pesthouse*, British author Jim Crace came to Los Angeles. During an event at the Central Library, he told the story of a phantom novel called *Useless America*, the rarest and most elusive of his works. *Useless America* is a book that never existed, the product of a computer error—or more accurately, a series of computer errors—that began when Crace signed the papers for *The Pesthouse*. At the time, he didn't have a title; to have something to put on the contract, he offered the only sentence he had written: "This used to be America." Somehow, that got transposed into *Useless America*, and so the ghostly book was born. "You know how computers are," Crace joked at the library. "They're promiscuous." Pretty soon, *Useless America* was listed at Amazon UK, where it rang up twenty-eight customer reviews. Crace began to order copies, eventually boosting his ranking to eighty-six, and when *The Pesthouse* finally appeared, Nan A. Talese, his American editor, decided to issue a gag version of *Useless America*, publishing seventy-five copies of a trade paperback edition, complete with dedication, a note on the text, and an array of fictional blurbs on the back. Inside, there is a two-page introduction by the author, explaining the origin of the work. The rest of the book is blank.

A blank book is a particular kind of symbol, a reflection of the possibilities literature provides. Yet as Crace understands, there is also something else at work here, especially when those possibilities are continually sublimated by faster, flashier entertainments, even as our ability to interact with them is inexorably changed. We cannot go back, although we do not yet know how to move forward, how to balance out the silence and the noise. Or maybe all those empty pages are a harbinger, an expression of just how much a book is worth. At the library, Crace raffled off a copy of *Useless America*, noting with an air of savage glee that collectors were offering a thousand dollars for it, signed. If you're looking for a subtext, a comment on the relative value of artifacts and words, Crace preferred to think of the situation in more pragmatic terms. A thousand dollars is a lot of money, and if the appeal of *Useless America* didn't exactly have to do with reading, it was an appeal nonetheless. "Sell it on eBay," he instructed the woman who won the raffle, after promising to sign the empty book.

One evening, Noah told me there was something I should see on Facebook. I was sitting at the computer (that all too common affliction) when he slid around me to log on. Within seconds, we were looking at a page called "I Attend Jay Gatsby's Parties," the creation of two Italian college students, and featuring more than forty-six thousand members, many of whom appeared to be high school kids assigned to read Fitzgerald's book. The wall was thick with comments, most tongue-in-cheek or, at least, elusively ironic. "So I'm hanging out with Catherine," one student wrote, "and her sister Myrtle comes by with Tom and some other dude. Everything was going fine until Myrtle starts to mouth off to Tom and he breaks her damn nose! I swear to God, Tom is such a tool!" *How cool is that?* I thought as Noah scrolled down, leapfrogging from post to post. There were photographs and videos, riffs, requests, and study questions, a virtual colloquy. I liked a three-panel comic strip in which Tom, clutching Daisy to his side, berates his rival: "You can never be like us, Gatsby. We're old money. . . . Old as *balls*." Noah preferred a thread that echoed the gossip of Gatsby's parties. "I heard he killed a man," it began, followed by three responses: "I heard he's related to Kaiser Wilhelm"; "I heard he's some big bootlegger"; and, "Well I heard he's some kind of harsh metaphor."

Both of us laughed at "Myrtle Gets Owned," a fifteen-second video reenacting the death of Myrtle, who is run down by Daisy in one of the novel's climactic scenes. Here, the vehicle was an SUV, not Gatsby's yellow roadster, and Myrtle was a mannequin, dressed in jeans and a sweater, on the side of a suburban street. As we watched, the SUV rolled across the screen, clipping the mannequin neatly and breaking it in half. Out of frame, we could hear the breathy laughter of the kid running the camera, a sound if not full of money then perhaps of loose change.

"I Attend Jay Gatsby's Parties" represents a particularly twenty-first-century extrapolation, the reader-author relationship writ large. As with my experience of *Sway* or *The Last Campaign*, it offers an externalized set of connections, but unlike a clip on YouTube, *this* material is interpretive, personal, truly interactive, a reflection of how we identify with the books we read. That it happens here in a collective manner, as if it were the expression of some type of hive mind, suggests a counterpoint to all the electronic distraction, a passage to an unexpected depth. It's not that the comments per se are so illuminating—you can't do much with "This is totally like the nerdiest group ever :) Brilliant!" . . . although I admire the enthusiasm—but rather the way they link to one another, building and changing, like an endless looping conversation, growing outward from the book.

The tone is almost directly opposite to that of the usual comments thread, a virtual discussion with a center, in which Fitzgerald's novel provokes a creative, as opposed to a vitriolic, response. As to why that is, perhaps it has to do with the age of so many participants. To look at their profile pictures, to read the unconstructed looseness of their language, is to be transported, in some strange sense, back to high school oneself. Many comments hint at assignments: "Opinions on the Valley of Ashes and Dr. T. J. Eckleburg," writes one correspondent, "go!" And yet, I can't help thinking, the difference is more than that, more a matter of engagement, even of self-respect. These are (or so I assume) real people, posting under real names, with photographs and links back to their Facebook pages. If nothing else, this creates an air of accountability. For a long time, I've thought of anonymity as the bane of the internet, allowing us to spew without recrimination or redress. It's one thing if you're Thomas Paine, wary of being prosecuted for sedition, and another if you're just an online coward, not willing to stand up for what you write. Given that, how can we not be gratified when high school students act more responsibly than their anonymous adult counterparts

(*FACTS getting in the way of your Socialist agenda??*)? Even more, how can we not be gratified by what "I Attend Jay Gatsby's Parties" has to tell us about literature and technology, about how the external feeds back into the internal, *about the way young readers read*?

When I was in college, a friend and I embarked on a similar kind of project, using technology to get inside a piece of literature. The book we chose was Franz Kafka's *The Metamorphosis*—then, as now, an abiding favorite—which we'd been assigned in a seminar on Kafka and Faulkner. I no longer recall the link our professor sought to draw between these two writers . . . or if, indeed, there was any link at all. But what I do remember is his willingness to let us play with the works we were discussing, his sense that, if literature were to remain a living force, we would all need to learn how to interact with it on our own terms. For us, that meant making a video, although to be honest, our original motivation was laziness. We were seniors, and we thought it would be easier than writing papers to produce an improvised adaptation of Kafka's novella, updated to the present day.

Here's how it worked: We gathered a group of friends and promised them beer if they would help us. We handed out parts and used another friend's apartment as a set. This was in West Philadelphia in the early

1980s, and the place was a lopsided railroad flat cut out of the second floor of a row house, up a narrow flight of stairs, with a small kitchen and an expansive bedroom in the front. We took it for granted that everyone had read the book, or at least knew the basics of the plot. *As Gregor Samsa awoke one morning from uneasy dreams he found himself transformed in his bed into a gigantic insect.* Is there a more evocative opening in all of literature? We weren't interested, however, in a straight adaptation, but rather in an *interpretation*, a video that would let us participate in a conversation, by which we could possess the narrative, reanimate it, while paying homage to a piece of writing that we loved. Both of us were fascinated by the fact that Kafka had asked Max Brod to burn his manuscripts when he knew full well that Brod would never do it: why had he not asked his father, who survived him, and who would have destroyed the writing in an instant, so fraught was his opinion of his son? Both of us were taken by the notion that, for Kafka, his characters were complicit in what happened to them: just as Josef K., in *The Trial*, must be guilty of something, if only being a part of a corrupt society, so, too, Gregor becomes an insect because in some sense he already is one, beaten down, beholden to his office and his family, scurrying through his life like some kind of bug. Both of us wanted the video to be funny: we thought (as I still do) that Kafka's humor is too often overlooked. The impetus was not dissimilar to that which had inspired the unfinished film about Milton, and, as I'd sought to do there, we chose to pepper our video with a succession of in-jokes about the author and his work.

As a result, our adaptation did not begin with Gregor's transformation, but in the days before. We filmed him trudging, insectlike, at 6:00 AM through Thirtieth Street Station, on his way to a commuter train. We improvised scenes of him with his sister and her boyfriend, a writer who declared his work should be destroyed, but who then exploded after Gregor tore a page from a notebook and held a match to it, shouting, "What are you doing? I was being *figurative.*" Later, when it came time for Gregor to change form, we overdubbed eerie electronic music and used a video effect that reversed the image so it looked like a negative. We zoomed in on the artifacts in his room, including a paperback of *The Metamorphosis* cracked open on his night table, as if he had been reading his own story into being.

Years later, I would stumble across Myron Brinig's *The Flutter of an Eyelid*, a 1933 novel set in Southern California in which the main character, a writer named Caslon Roanoke, gradually comes to realize that much of the action he is describing occurs only after he has "written" it, the narrative growing out of his dreams. This, of course, is a vivid metaphor for what every writer—or reader—does. We take language and put it through a personal metamorphosis, reacting to it, reinventing it, making it our own. (*The reader becomes the book.*) The best books are those most open to such a process, the ones that seem to grow along with us, allowing us to inhabit them in different ways at different times. *Stop-Time, On the Road, The Sound and the Fury, Slouching Towards Bethlehem, The Metamorphosis*: I've read and reread these books, as a teenager and in my twenties, thirties, and forties, and each time I do, they illuminate something new for me, some new point of view or perspective, not just about the authors or their stories but about myself. How, for instance, when I was twenty-five and passing through North Platte, could I have read *On the Road* as the story of two lost boys, Sal and Dean, Jack and Neal, adrift not just in the immensity of America but of the universe? I had to be older, to have passed through what they were experiencing, to see it from the other side. The same is true of *The Metamorphosis*, with its vision of existential futility, in which for me now, Gregor's fate seems more expansive, not just his but that of all of us. Even *The Great Gatsby* becomes a mirror, reflecting back the things we need to see. Soap opera, meditation on America, or a closer read on corruption and the loss of love; what you find there depends on who, or where, you are.

In that sense, "I Attend Jay Gatsby's Parties" illustrates a three-dimensional relationship to literature *in action*, a series of real-time responses to Fitzgerald's book. As with our video of *The Metamorphosis*, the posts can be snarky, silly; what is intimacy, after all, if you can't poke fun at the source of your affection, at that obscure object of desire? Yet in the midst of that, there are hints of something deeper, some connection that extends beneath the surface—of both the novel and the Facebook group. When one student writes, "I feel like Fitzgerald is just fucking with everyone. . . . I can't see any man intentionally putting all of that symbolism in a book," it spawns a discussion twenty-four comments long. At the core here is not just one student's frustration, but the essence of how we think about fiction, what we expect literature to do. Scrolling down the thread, I am reminded again of the fallacies of the classroom, of the belief that there is a right or wrong way to read a novel, that we can decipher a book as if it were an extended piece of code. I am reminded again of my frustration studying *Lord of the Flies* in junior high school, my sense that I was being taught to misread it, that my teacher was finding things that weren't there.

"So Gatsby and Daisy are an egg?" a girl asks, then answers her own question: "Oh wait . . . West Egg, East Egg. Man this shit is easy to make up." Later, the kid who started the conversation advises another student on how to take a test. "Just BS your way using 'American Dream is a lie,'" he writes, "'Gatsby's obsession with Daisy' and the [difference] between the wealthy and the [nouveau] riche. . . . You'll be sure to get an A." It's a cynical remark, but not about the novel, just about the way it's taught. And in that moment, these Facebook friends, these comment posters, get at something more real, something closer to the flow of literature, than a more academic approach to reading ever will.

Of course, in order to understand that flow, you have to read the book. That, too, is at the heart of "I Attend Jay Gatsby's Parties," and the first few times I visited, it gnawed at me like a promise that had gone unkept. By the time he introduced me to the page, Noah had finished *The Great Gatsby*, turning in his annotations and an essay on the novel's larger themes. After our brief conversation in the car, we had not discussed the book again, except for his comment on the writing in the final chapters and how beautiful he thought it was. I had been released, no need to swim out and get him, no need to carry him home. And yet, *The Great Gatsby* remained on my nightstand, as if in silent rebuke to my inability to make it to the end. I was stalled seventy pages from the finish, with Nick having just returned from, yes, attending one of Gatsby's parties, and all the connections, or disconnections, established and in place. Just before I left off, Gatsby had lamented his failure to impress Daisy:

> "She didn't like it," he said immediately.
>
> "Of course she did."
>
> "She didn't like it," he insisted. "She didn't have a good time."
>
> He was silent and I guessed at his unutterable depression.
>
> "I feel far away from her," he said. "It's hard to make her understand."
>
> "You mean about the dance?"
>
> "The dance?" He dismissed all the dances he had given with a snap of his fingers. "Old sport, the dance is unimportant."

Now, he was stuck there, both of them were stuck there, waiting for me to see their story through. Thinking about it, I realized I had been wrong about who was at risk of drowning; it had not been Noah, but rather Gatsby, Nick, and me. Noah had long since returned to the safety of the boat, but we were still out in the water; we were still at sea. As for beating on against the current, it was entirely up to me.

E arly in the spring of 2010, over breakfast, a friend showed me her iPad. This was in April, only a week or two after the device had debuted; Apple was, as they say, moving units, but this had not yet translated into any real-world effect that I could see. One of the conundrums of e-readers, in my limited experience, is how few of them I come across in daily life. I know the statistics, know about the buzz they generate, but I can probably count on both hands the number of times I've encountered one in actual use. Partly, I suppose, that has to do with living in Los Angeles, where, as Didion has written, "a good part of any day . . . is spent driving, alone, through streets devoid of meaning to the driver, which is one reason the place exhilarates some people, and floods others with an amorphous unease." This is a city defined by private, not public, space, in which I rarely ride the bus or the subway, rarely go to the park anymore now that I have older kids. I don't have as much opportunity for the serendipitous encounter as I might in a more traditional city such as New York. Still, even when I find myself around masses of people, e-readers don't yet seem a significant part of the mix. I notice them when I fly, in terminals and on airplanes, but the numbers are small, in ones and twos, much less than you'd expect. Not long ago, I spent a week in Palm Springs and saw one woman, once, reading on a Kindle while sitting beside the pool. I have never seen a Nook or a Sony Reader, except as a display model, and, until my friend took out her iPad and offered me a demonstration, I had never seen one of those outside the Apple store. What this means, I think, is that there is still a certain disconnect between where the culture is and where it's going, between the machines that appear likely to define the future of reading and how we use them (or don't use them) in the present tense.

As it turns out, I was enraptured by the iPad; I'm no Luddite, after all. I love my iPod, love my BlackBerry, love the limitless reach technology offers when I don't allow myself to get lost. Sitting at the table, I opened the Marvel Comics app and scrolled through an issue of *X-Men*, admiring the digital clarity of the art. I zoomed in on individual images, read part of the story frame by frame as if it were an animation, somewhere between the movie screen and the page. Next, my friend showed me the iBook version of A. A. Milne's *Winnie-the-Pooh*, which had come pre-loaded as a tease. As I navigated the story with a succession of finger swipes, I saw for the first time an e-book that *looked like a book*, with page numbers and illustrations, an attention to design. I've had a Kindle for a while now, but I rarely use it because the interface is inhospitable to me. I think in pages, not in screens; I like the idea of the book as object, of the book as artifact, of reading as a three-dimensional, tactile experience, in which the way a text looks or feels or even smells has an influence over how, or whether, I engage.

In an August 3, 2009, piece for *The New Yorker*, Nicholson Baker addresses this question, noting that, when it comes to reading, the Kindle 2 (the same model I own) has all the charm of a Nexis search. "The problem," Baker writes, "was not that the screen was in black-and-white; if it had really been black-and-white, that would have been fine. The problem was that the screen was gray. And it wasn't just gray; it was a greenish, sickly gray. A postmortem gray. The resiz-able typeface, Monotype Caecilia, appeared as a darker gray. Dark gray on paler greenish gray was the palette of the Amazon Kindle." I agree; among the things the Kindle makes me long for is the clarity of ink on paper, or as Baker describes it, "sharp black letters laid out like lacquered chopsticks on a clean tablecloth." But even more, the Kindle lacks what, for want of a better word, we might call the *charm* of reading, the intangibles that give a book its *bookness*, as it were. Here's Baker again, framing the issue neatly:

> Yes, you can definitely read things on the Kindle. And I did. Bits of things at first. I read some of De Quincey's *Confessions*, some of Robert Benchley's *Love Conquers All*, and some of several versions of Kipling's *The Jungle Book*. I squeezed no new joy from these great books, though. The Gluyas Williams drawings were gone from the Benchley, and even the wasp passage in "Do Insects Think?" just wasn't the same in Kindle gray. I did an experiment. I found the Common Reader reprint edition of *Love Conquers All* and read the very same wasp passage. I laughed: *ha-ha*. Then I went back to the Kindle 2 and read the wasp passage again. No laugh. Of course, by then I'd read the passage three times, and it wasn't that funny anymore. But the point is that it wasn't funny the first time I came to it, when it was enscreened on the Kindle. Monotype Caecilia was grim and Calvinist; it

had a way of reducing everything to arbitrary heaps of words.

For Baker, there were other issues. You might be able to store up to fifteen hundred titles on your Kindle—a good-sized personal library, enough to read a book a week, every week, for thirty years— but you can't lend them, give them away, print them, email them to a friend. Except for the iPad and the iPod (*there's an app for that*), you can't read them on a competing machine. "Here's what you buy when you buy a Kindle book," Baker tells us. "You buy the right to display a grouping of words in front of your eyes for your private use with the aid of an electronic display device approved by Amazon. . . . They are closed clumps of digital code that only one purchaser can own. A copy of a Kindle book dies with its possessor." This, of course, is the whole idea, to create a closed loop between store and reader, which raises not-so-subtle questions about engagement and control. Similar questions also mark the relationship between publishers and writers, which is nothing if not proprietary; that's the nature of a contract, after all. The difference is that once a print book goes to market, it slips the bounds of this dynamic, existing as a physical object on its own terms. For Amazon, the circle is much tighter, allowing for greater levels of control. That's good for business, since the more hegemony the company exerts, the better off it is. For the culture, though, books serve as a collective soul, a memory bank, bigger than mere commerce, not only to be bought and sold. When we can't share them, directly, one-to-one, our common informational heritage is compromised.

It didn't help that, just a week or so before Baker's article appeared, Amazon remotely deleted digital copies of George Orwell's *1984* and *Animal Farm* from customers' Kindles after learning that the electronic publisher of these works did not have the rights to them. Setting aside for the moment the matter of irony, or public relations—the decision was a fiasco on both fronts and was rapidly reversed after a public outcry in which the online bookseller found itself compared to the censors in *1984* who rewrite history by consigning offending news items to an incinerator chute known as the memory hole—this suggests some fundamental issues regarding the nature of information systems and the challenges of an electronic model for intellectual and literary life. Such concerns are hardly exclusive to Amazon. In June 2010, Apple, citing a companywide antiporn policy as justification, coerced the creators of a webcomic version of *Ulysses* to redraw several panels in which characters appeared nude before their adaptation could be sold in the iPad App Store. Here, too, the irony comes fast and furious. As Kevin Kelleher wrote at TheBigMoney.com: "Somewhere, James Joyce must be laughing at Steve Jobs. . . . As everyone who took a modern lit class in college knows, *Ulysses* was banned from publication in the United States because of a scene in which Leopold Bloom masturbates on a beach while fireworks burst nearby. The courts eventually decided the episode wasn't obscene because it didn't promote lust." What's next, you have to wonder? *Howl*? *Lady Chatterley's Lover*? *Tropic of Cancer*? Are we destined to replay all the censorship battles of the last seventy-five years in the electronic arena, long after they have been won for print? It may be a brave new world, as web evangelists such as Clay Shirky like to claim, but on these terms, at least, it seems that the future is looking an awful lot like the past.

To be fair, that's part of the shakeout as literature makes the shift to the electronic realm. In much the same way as Amazon, Apple backtracked on *Ulysses* (as well as on a related issue involving an adaptation of Oscar Wilde's *The Importance of Being Earnest*) almost immediately, asking the developers "to resubmit their original material." In an update on his post, Kelleher cites an email from Apple spokesperson Trudy Muller: "We made a mistake. When the art panel edits of the *Ulysses Seen* app and the graphic novel adaptation of

Oscar Wilde's *Importance of Being Earnest* app were brought to our attention, we offered the developers the opportunity to resubmit their original drawings and update their apps." Both works were made available in unexpurgated form. For that reason, and despite all commentary to the contrary—"Apple continues to run amok censoring iPad/iPhone apps," wrote Ryan Chittum on the *Columbia Journalism Review* website—this seems less a matter of censorship than one of stupidity, or bad business, the result of a cognitive disconnect. The iPad or the Kindle may be devices for reading, but they are also commodities to be bought and sold. If the same is true of books, the publishing industry has long operated under the illusion that it is different, a gentlemen's (or gentlewomen's) business, in which ideas, not commerce, are common currency. Whether or not this is the case (it isn't) is not the issue; what's important is that it has engendered a set of shared ideals or beliefs. When it comes to e-reading, however, other influences, other belief systems come into play.

Partly, this has to do with economics: publishers signing on with one platform and not the other, different models by which writers get paid. But even more, it has to do with culture and how it changes and grows. Baker's right: the Kindle (or the iPad, for that matter) privatizes the most public aspects of reading, reducing the conversation to a soliloquy. For all its storage capabilities, if that's the only way you do your reading, no one can come into your house and peruse your shelves. Not only that, but even the contents of this virtual library are subject to the very sorts of artificial restrictions—what's available in the iBookstore or the Kindle store—that the technology revolution was meant to overthrow. Out in the world, there are any number of places to buy books, new or old, including the internet, where I have found a whole host of things (Vonnegut's early book of stories *Canary in a Cathouse*, Denis Johnson's poetry collection *The Veil*) that I'd spent years looking for. For the iPad or the Kindle, I can't find the most common titles: *Stop-Time*, *The White Album*, anything by Faulkner other than *New Orleans Sketches*. This, of course, is changing by the minute, but even by the most optimistic standards, it will be years before e-book retailers catch up. For Baker, this provokes a comparison with his own bookshelves, packed with the effluvia of a lifetime of reading:

> Back home, I spent an hour standing in front of some fiction bookcases, checking on titles. There is no Amazon Kindle version of *The Jewel in the Crown*. There's no Kindle of Jean

Stafford, no Vladimir Nabokov, no *Flaubert's Parrot*, no *Remains of the Day*, no *Perfume* by Patrick Suskind, no Bharati Mukherjee, no Margaret Drabble, no Graham Greene except a radio script, no David Leavitt, no Bobbie Ann Mason's *In Country*, no Pynchon, no Tim O'Brien, no *Swimming-Pool Library*, no Barbara Pym, no Saul Bellow, no Frederick Exley, no *World According to Garp*, no *Catch-22*, no *Breakfast at Tiffany's*, no *Portnoy's Complaint*, no *Henry and Clara*, no Lorrie Moore, no *Edwin Mullhouse*, no *Clockwork Orange*.

Such a list is, in many ways, akin to Conroy's, a mapping of the reader's inner life. But there is more to it, since if e-books privatize the public elements of reading, then the physical library effectively does the reverse. I have thousands of books in my house, arranged alphabetically by author, with no attention to subject or style. This reflects, I'm sure, some funda- mental things about me: a disbelief in genre (which I've always regarded as a set of boxes by which to catego- rize writing, whereas writing, or *good* writing, should stand against categorization in any form); a fascination with the unexpected correlations that fire across the shelves like synapses, one triggering another in a loose chain of associations, of serendipity. What do Aristotle, Karen Armstrong, Antonin Artaud, Herbert Asbury, Margaret Atwood, Augustine, and Ken Auletta have in common? Nothing, except they sit together in my bookcase, reflecting my interests, tastes, desires, even aspirations—a manifestation of my mind. Why does my old Signet paperback of *Three by Flannery O'Connor* (*Wise Blood*, *The Violent Bear It Away*, *A Good Man Is Hard to Find*) continue to resonate even after *Wise Blood* emptied out for me? Because of how the book, the *object*, recalls my experience of reading it, nineteen years old, as lonely and alienated as Hazel Motes, waiting in a Flagstaff, Arizona, motel room for daybreak, when I would board an Amtrak train bound for Chicago and then Massachusetts, to see my family for the first time in nearly a year. Here, we find a different kind of memory hole, the hole of individual memory, the way our books reflect identity. This is equally true, I think, of those we haven't read, or are currently reading, or will never read at all. Every library worth the name contains dozens, if not hundreds, of books that fit these criteria, that speak to where we wish to go as much as where we've been. Remember Weil: "One must believe in the reality of Time" . . . and this is one of the most powerful gifts a library has to offer, to represent not just our histories but also our imaginations, until past, present, and future begin to take shape in three dimensions, to occupy a space that, while outside us, stands in some significant fashion for who we are.

In an April 15, 2010, "Editorial Notebook" piece in the *New York Times*, Verlyn Klinkenborg writes:

> As always, I am reading several books at a time—actually, several stacks. One is the stack of heirloom books by my bed, which begins with the engaging and soon-to-be-published *Camel* by Robert Irwin and works haphazardly outward to Rose Macaulay's *The Towers of Trebizond* and Bronislaw Malinowski's *A Diary in the Strict Sense of the Term.*
>
> And then there is a virtual stack of e-books. There is Alvin Kernan's *Crossing the Line*, which I'm reading on my laptop via ebrary. I'm using other e-book software, like Kindle for the Mac and Stanza. My iPad is on its way.
>
> In one way or another, I've been reading on a computer ever since it meant looking at green phosphor pixels against a black background. And I love the prospect of e-reading —the immediacy it offers, the increasing

wealth of its resources. But I'm discovering,
too, a hidden property in printed books, one
of the reasons I will always prefer them. They
do nothing.

What's interesting about these observations is
how they encapsulate both the pros and the cons of
electronic reading. (*The test of a first-rate intelligence
is the ability to hold two opposed ideas in the mind
at the same time.*) For all that he embraces technology, Klinkenborg worries about interactivity and its
discontents: "A paper book," he tells us, "aids my concentration by offering to do nothing else but lie open in
front of me, mute until I rest my eyes upon it. It won't
search for a flight or balance my checkbook or play
an episode of *The Larry Sanders Show* or catch up on
Google Reader. It won't define a word, unless the book
happens to be a lexicon or have a glossary." I worry
about this also—and yet, implicit in our concerns is an
understanding that the conversation has changed. As
readers, we are in a period of evolution. Although we
still can't multitask within an e-book, that moment is
coming . . . fast. Indeed, at the edges of the culture, we
are already adjusting our ideas of what books are and
how they operate.

In November 2009, Rick Moody, in conjunction with the multiplatform literary journal *Electric Literature* (*there's an app for that*) published a story called "Some Contemporary Characters" in 153 increments on Twitter, one tweet per hour for nearly a week. If the story didn't quite work, or take full advantage of the medium, it might still be read as a harbinger. "I'm making up the form," Moody told the *Wall Street Journal*, "making up how to use Twitter to advance story structure, and that there are not handholds yet for exactly how to do that. There are handholds for how to pace a *New Yorker* story, or how to make a short fiction collection, but there are, as yet, no handholds for how to pace a Twitter story, or how to sustain interest over the course of days." Nor are there handholds for more ambitious multimedia projects, including those that involve experimental software such as Sophie, originally developed by the Institute for the Future of the Book and now administered by the University of Southern California's School of Cinematic Arts, which released a "significantly revised and improved" version in December 2009. Sophie is an open-source program designed to allow writers and other artists "to combine text, images, video, and sound quickly and simply, but with precision and sophistication." What does this mean? Imagine a text in which, rather than footnotes, hyperlinks take us to sources and other secondary material. Imagine that, instead of static images, we can embed video or audio directly in the work. Such a project would look like a book—designed, laid out in pages, linearly structured, to be read front to back—yet it would also incorporate the best of technological innovation, not for its own sake but *in the service of the narrative*. The catch, of course, is that it would not exist in print, but only digitally.

Again, this brings us face-to-face with the core philosophical issue—is it still reading if we do it on the screen? On the one hand, hyperlinks and other electronic innovations can't help but break the flow of language, interrupting our immersion in the word. In *The Shallows*, Carr cites a 2009 article by Patricia Greenfield, a UCLA developmental psychologist who examined the results of "more than fifty studies of the effects of different types of media on people's intelligence and learning ability." Her conclusion? That "our growing use of the Net and other screen-based technologies" has undermined "our capacities for the kind of 'deep processing' that underpins 'mindful knowledge acquisition, inductive analysis, critical thinking, imagination, and reflection.'" For Carr, this suggests that "the Net is making us smarter . . . only if we define intelligence by the Net's own standards. If we take a broader and more traditional view of intelligence—if we think about the depth of our thought, rather than just its speed—we have to come to a different and considerably darker conclusion." *If we take a broader and more traditional view of intelligence* . . . he's referring here to a density of attention, in which "the reading of a sequence of printed pages was valuable not just for the knowledge readers acquired from the author's words but for the way those words set off intellectual vibrations within their own minds. In the quiet spaces opened up by the prolonged, undistracted reading of a book, people made their own associations, drew their own inferences and analogies, fostered their own ideas. They thought deeply as they read deeply." Carr continues:

> Even the earliest silent readers recognized the striking change in their consciousness that took place as they immersed themselves in the pages of a book. The medieval bishop Isaac of Syria described how, whenever he read to himself, "as in a dream, I enter a state when my sense and thoughts are concentrated. Then, when with prolonging of this silence the turmoil of memories is stilled in my heart, ceaseless waves of joy are sent to me by inner thoughts, beyond expectation suddenly arising to delight my heart." Reading a book

was a meditative act, but it didn't involve a clearing of the mind. It involved a filling, or replenishing, of the mind. Readers disengaged their attention from the outward flow of passing stimuli in order to engage it more deeply with an inward flow of words, ideas, and emotions. That was—and is—the essence of the unique mental process of deep reading. It was the technology of the book that made this "strange anomaly" in our psychological history possible. The brain of the book reader was more than a literate brain. It was a literary brain.

But what if "our brain's plasticity," as Carr puts it, cuts both ways? This is part of the argument, that brain function is not fixed but fluid, that "our neurological system . . . 'with its branches and transmitters and ingeniously spanned gaps, has an improvised quality that seems to mirror the unpredictability of thought itself.'" We are adaptable, in other words, as our efforts to frame a common territory between technology and literature shows. Already, we read in multiple ways on multiple platforms, depending on where we are and what we want. In addition to the books that fill my shelves, I regularly access online resources such as

Project Gutenberg and Google Books. For all my antip-
athy to the Kindle, I've loaded my iPod with hundreds of
titles, from the *Complete Works of William Shakespeare*
to *The Federalist Papers* to, yes, *The Great Gatsby*. Does
this mean I'm reading on the machine more? Yes and
no. The fact that I *can*, however—that, on a small hand-
held device, which fits into my pocket, I can carry mil-
lions of words from across the ages—makes me feel as if
I'm standing on the edge of something, albeit something
I don't yet fully understand.

Of course, the books I've downloaded to my iPod
are not new to me, but rather works I know from other
formats, from the physical, as well as the virtual, world.
In that sense, e-reading remains an ancillary activity, less about discovery than reassurance of a kind.
This, Baker notes, is one appeal of the iPod, which
offers ease of access "when you wake up at 3 AM and you
need big, sad, well-placed words to tumble slowly into
the basin of your mind." The sensation he describes is
familiar: "Hold it a few inches from your face with the
words enlarged and the screen's brightness slider bar
slid to its lowest setting, and read for ten or fifteen minutes. . . . After a while, your thoughts will drift off to
the unused siding where the old tall weeds are, and the
string of curving words will toot a mournful toot and
pull ahead." That is what it's like to read a book under

the covers, while holding a flashlight up to the page. It reflects one of my most common memories of childhood, another kind of neural pathway, an experience etched deeply into my brain. Something similar occurs with the iPad, or with software such as Sophie, both of which evoke an essential booklike sensibility within the digital realm. It doesn't seem like too much of a stretch to suggest that what we have here is an example of art influencing technology, a back-and-forth that has its roots in our relationship to written language and then extrapolates outward, to the screen.

This, too, cuts both ways, reflecting the plasticity not just of our brains but also of our creativity. It's not only Moody or *Electric Literature*; all writing is (must be) changing to reflect the exigencies of the digital world. As early as 1999, Sylvia Brownrigg's novel *The Metaphysical Touch* integrated newsgroup posts and emails into the fiber of its narrative, as a strategy for investigating the relationship between technology and intimacy. "It was quiet," Brownrigg observes of electronic communication, "it didn't require immediate response, as a voice on the telephone did. . . . But it didn't require a physical body of print on paper. Ontologically, email was not in any recognizable category: neither voice nor paper, neither pure mind nor pure matter." Eleven years later, Jennifer Egan's novel

A Visit from the Goon Squad includes a chapter written in PowerPoint, from the perspective of a twelve-year-old girl trying to navigate the emotional subcurrents that buffet her family.

To look at this material in print is to engage it through one kind of filter; rendered in black and gray, devoid of electronic components, it's interesting if a bit abstracted, the representation more than the expression of an idea. To see it online, however—Egan has posted a multimedia version on her website—is to be asked to consider narrative in a new way. Telling a story in seventy-six frames, with snippets of rock songs as a soundtrack, the chapter literally teaches us how to read it as we go along. One early panel breaks down the family in a Venn diagram, with four separate circles, one each for the narrator, her brother, and her parents, overlapping a larger central circle labeled, "Us." Later, an empty word balloon appears beneath the heading "A Pause While We Stand on the Deck." Both pages evoke the silence, the distance, that can encompass us even (or especially) in the presence of our loved ones, and it makes me want to read Egan's novel on a device where I could toggle between text and internet . . . or where the multimedia components came embedded directly into the book itself. Perhaps the next generation of iPad will have that ability, although for that to happen, *A Visit from the Goon Squad* would have to be available from the iBookstore, which it isn't yet. You *can* buy it for the Kindle, but reading it on one is a static experience, with neither the capabilities of multimedia nor the efficacy of the printed page.

On the one hand, this might not appear to have a lot to do with literature, despite the presence of the words. It might seem more of a stunt, a gimmick, a way to attract attention in a distracted world. And yet, again, what is literature if not a gimmick, an illusion, in which we take the raw materials at our disposal (ink, paper, binary code, perspective) and fashion out of them a contrivance, an invention, an elaborate shadow play? The miracle is that we can believe any of it, that these tools, as imperfect as they are, can stir us into trusting something that is, on the most basic level, not actually there. As for PowerPoint, it's just another option, one that emerges directly from the world in which we live. During a May 2010 panel at BookExpo America, the publishing industry's annual book fair and trade show, Egan explained the impetus for her experiment:

> I had never used PowerPoint and didn't own it.
> I normally write fiction by hand. So it took me
> some months of trial and error and reading
> in the genre—mostly corporate narratives of

profit and loss and restructuring—to understand that I was not trying to write fiction
in bullet points or to illustrate the action as
in a graphic novel. What I needed to do was
find the internal structure of each fictional
moment and reveal it visually. . . . One of the
projects of modernism was to try to capture
the simultaneity of consciousness, where perception is happening on multiple fronts, and
a moment can be read many different ways.
Slides made that experience literally possible.
I could let information float on a screen, often
without a clear order, so that multiple readings
were guaranteed.

What this suggests (to me, anyway) is that the most
authentic e-reading experience may be one in which,
like Egan's online PowerPoint presentation, the capabilities of the machine are brought into play. And yet, it's
telling that she refers to modernism, not just because
writers such as Joyce and Pound would have gone mad
for contemporary technology (can you imagine *Ulysses*
in hypertext? Or *The Cantos*?), but also because,
despite all aspirations to the contrary, modernism did
not eradicate everything that came before. "We have
evolved a new cosmogony of literature," Henry Miller

wrote in *Tropic of Cancer*. "It is to be a new Bible—*The Last Book*. All those who have anything to say will say it here—*anonymously*. After us not another book—not for a generation, at least." Joyce may have had similar ambitions—"the whatness of allbook," in Miller's pointed phrase, a sense that all literary convention was being put to rest—but history, as it turns out, was not a nightmare from which he could awake. Instead, modernism became just the latest layer in an ongoing conversation, a conversation that began in Mesopotamia ten thousand years ago.

Less than a century later, modernism, too, has been superseded as literature continues to evolve. The same is true of e-books, which no more displace physical books, or the act of reading them, than modernism severed the narrative cord. And yet, they also leave us with a number of open-ended questions about the bond between a reader and a writer, about what reading is and what it will become. It hasn't been so long since I read *Sway* and *The Last Campaign* in conjunction with those YouTube videos, yet my discomfort at sidestepping the boundaries of the book is one the culture has, for all intents and purposes, moved beyond. That moment is past; we've gone from a situation in which technology allows us to enhance a book *after it's been written* to one in which authors such as Moody or Egan adapt it in the framing of their texts. Technology, in other words, is now a matter of aesthetics, of intention. But if this suggests a new approach to writing, what's important is that we have the agency, that as readers, we get to decide.

So as the market for e-books continues to grow, and more writers think—really *think*—about technology as a métier, here's a little fantasy in which I like to indulge on occasion, a game of what-if, another way of thinking about the neural pathways, as it were. What if the e-book is a catalyst for reconnection, by engaging our fascination with technology to stir long-form reading, by integrating deep concentration with the lure of the machine? What if the e-book is the means by which we start to get beneath the fragmentation, the scattering of attention, the drift that marks so much of our digital life? I say this as someone who doesn't do a lot of electronic reading. (I recently charged my Kindle for the first time in months.) I say this in spite of all the issues, the problems over Orwell and *Ulysses*, the unavailability of such a wide variety of work. I say this knowing that the e-reader changes the nature of the conversation, and yet, I can't help but feel hopeful about the buzz these devices generate, all those people reading books on-screen. The process is familiar, as familiar as Baker turning to his iPod in the middle of a sleepless night. What we read might be a series of tweets, or it might include a PowerPoint chart. It might be an old book, newly digitized. It might have illustrations, might involve some interactive bells and whistles, as in the iPad edition of *Alice's Adventures in Wonderland*, where, as Klinkenborg points out, "mushrooms . . . tumble out of the upper margin" of the page. But what all of this shares is a certain primacy of the text, a sense that, enhanced or otherwise, reading can exist in a variety of different forms.

I finally finished rereading *The Great Gatsby* on a Thursday in May. I was alone, in a borrowed office at the University of California, Irvine, where I had been teaching a weekly literary journalism seminar. Just below the surface of almost every classroom meeting was the issue of where, of how, of what to do with this material now that the venues for long-form journalism have largely disappeared. We looked at an array of models—Didion's essays "Slouching Towards Bethlehem" and "The White Album," Norman Mailer's *Miami and the Siege of Chicago*, David Foster Wallace's "A Supposedly Fun Thing I'll Never Do Again"—all of

which had originally appeared in mass-market pub-
lications such as *Harper's* and the *Saturday Evening
Post*. These were long pieces, meaty pieces, pieces that
required the stamina of real reading, that necessitated
taking a vertical plunge. What was the contemporary
analogue? Was it still possible to do this type of work?
To illustrate a different set of options, I had the students
read Joe Sacco's *Footnotes in Gaza*, a four-hundred-
page journalistic comic book about two 1956 incidents
in the Gaza Strip, and Jason Motlagh's "Sixty Hours of
Terror," a twenty-thousand-word hour-by-hour account
of the November 2008 Mumbai terrorist attacks, published over four days on the blog of the literary journal
Virginia Quarterly Review. I assigned *Common Sense*,
talked about Paine's embrace of the vernacular, not just
in regard to language but also in his use of the pamphlet, his willingness to operate along what was then
the technological cutting edge. We discussed e-books
and online reading, conjectured about all the ways the
landscape might or might not change. What if, I asked,
citing Motlagh as an example, computers or e-readers
could be framed as a new kind of pamphlet: portable,
accessible, effective for both long and short work,
unbound by the burdensome economies of print?

Of course, as is also true of my fantasy about
the e-book, I'm not sure what I really think. In the

classroom, I was mostly trying to suggest possibilities. Still, I can't pretend that the notion of an electroliterary utopia, in which every book that has ever been written (and, perhaps, every book that has *never* been written) are all equally available, doesn't make my stomach roll and my sphincter tighten in anticipation, just as they did when I used to wander into Spring Street Books. It would be like having access to some vast Borgesian library . . . although the iterations inherent in such a project can be overwhelming, even dangerous, as Borges himself recognized. His 1941 short story "The Library of Babel" imagines a universe in the form of a boundless library, "composed of an indefinite and perhaps infinite number of hexagonal galleries." Such a place is self-contained and inviolable, offering us no choice but to confront our insignificance; it is a closed system, with no particular need for us at all. "Man, the imperfect librarian," Borges writes, "may be the product of chance or of malevolent demiurgi; the universe, with its elegant endowment of shelves, of enigmatical volumes, of inexhaustible stairways for the traveler and latrines for the seated librarian, can only be the work of a god." More apropos, this perfection leaves us at the end point of the possible, an end point with no resolution and no beginning, no way to catalogue it all. As Borges writes:

> *In the vast Library there are no two identical
> books.* . . . The Library is total and . . . its
> shelves register all the possible combinations
> of the twenty-odd orthographical symbols (a
> number which, though extremely vast, is not
> infinite): Everything: the minutely detailed
> history of the future, the archangels' auto-
> biographies, the faithful catalogues of the
> Library, thousands and thousands of false
> catalogues, the demonstration of the fallacy
> of those catalogues, the demonstration of
> the fallacy of the true catalogue, the Gnostic
> gospel of Basilides, the commentary on that
> gospel, the commentary on the commentary
> on that gospel, the true story of your death,
> the translation of every book in all languages,
> the interpolations of every book in all books.

In an essay originally posted in 1999 on the newsgroup rec.arts.books, Christopher Rollason recasts
"The Library of Babel" in contemporary terms. "This,
certainly," he writes, "could be read as prefiguring the
inhabitants of today's or tomorrow's world of virtual
information, with their consciousness saturated by an
endless flow of cyberdata." Indeed, because the library
contains not just every book, actual or potential, but

also "every possible combination of letters in every language" (*all the possible combinations of the twenty-odd orthographical symbols*), Rollason suggests that "the great majority of the books are completely useless, and statistically it would be a remarkable feat to find even one 'real,' actually readable book in months searching the shelves—and even then, the chances of its content being of any use or interest to the seeker would be minimal."

What "The Library of Babel" evokes is an extreme image of saturation, the place where possibility tips into overload. For Borges, this was a metaphor, but as Rollason's essay indicates, we now live, at least to some extent, in Borges's world. What we need is silence—not to disconnect but as a respite, to uncover a little piece of stillness in the din. This is what I found on Thursday afternoons in Irvine. At five o'clock, after class was over, I would buy a cup of coffee and retreat upstairs to my borrowed office to wait out the rush-hour traffic before driving back to Los Angeles. Ostensibly, these were my office hours, but almost no one ever came. Instead, I would sit there, in a room containing the most generic commercial furniture (two desks, two chairs, a metal filing cabinet), and I would read. Sometimes, I read student papers, trying to get a jump on the following week. Once or twice, I read a book I was going to review. I brought *The Great Gatsby* with me a few times before I actually got to it, toward the end of the quarter, on a quiet afternoon. Outside, students called back and forth to one another as they passed along the main pathway of the campus; above the tree line, the light began to grow hazy, diffuse, in places almost pixilated, what Lawrence Weschler in his 1998 essay "L.A. Glows" refers to as "the late-afternoon light of Los Angeles—golden pink off the bay through the smog and onto the palm fronds."

I read quickly and without interruption, almost as if I were a teenager again. First, I went back to refresh myself, to get situated. I paged through a few scenes (Tom and Myrtle drinking in the upper Manhattan apartment, Daisy and Gatsby meeting for tea at Nick's small house) and began. "It was when curiosity about Gatsby was at its highest," Fitzgerald opens chapter 7, "that the lights in his house failed to go on one Saturday night—and, as obscurely as it had begun, his career as Trimalchio was over." That's an almost perfect first sentence—fluid, light to the touch, full of promise, of insinuation—and it carried me back into the text. If, when I had first returned to *Gatsby*, I had done so with an agenda (to help Noah, to steer him back toward shore), now I was reading purely for the sake of reading, for the play of the sentences, for the flow of the narrative. I felt myself enter Fitzgerald's language, felt its lilt, its music, carry me away.

And here again is what reading has to offer: the blurring of the boundaries that divide us, that keep us separate and apart. And here again, I find myself in the thrall of that interior communion, as Fitzgerald inhabits me and I animate him. I do not believe that anything is lasting; all of it will be taken from us in the end. Chaos, entropy . . . the best that we can hope for are a few transcendent moments, in which we bridge the gap of our loneliness and come together with another human being. This is what reading has always meant to me and what, even more, it means to me now. Sitting in that empty office in Irvine, experiencing the confrontation at the Plaza, the death of Myrtle, Gatsby's tragic end, I felt as rapt and quiet, as *fulfilled*, as I have ever been. "They were careless people, Tom and Daisy," Fitzgerald writes in the novel's last pages, "they smashed up things and creatures and then retreated back into their money or their vast carelessness or whatever it was that kept them together, and let other people clean up the mess they had made." He's right, of course, and yet, in his portrayal of the precise quality of their carelessness, a kind of empathy is made. Not for them so much as for those around them . . . or maybe, in some strange sense, for all of us. Either way, the ability of the writing to connect reminds me once again of Conroy (*the real world dissolved and I was free to drift in fantasy, living a thousand lives, each one more powerful, more accessible, and more real than my own*) and his deft encapsulation of the reader's art.

For Conroy, this was all a matter of reflex; "I read very fast, uncritically, and without retention," as he recalls. For me, the experience was more heightened, perhaps because I couldn't take it for granted anymore. Sitting in Irvine, finishing *The Great Gatsby*, I began to understand that I'd been given something, a respite, a way of reading that felt pure. This seems obvious, silly even, but it bears repeating, especially in an age when all our time seems parceled out, accounted for. This is the burden of technology, that we are never disconnected, never out of touch. And yet, reading is, by its nature, a strategy for displacement, for pulling back from the circumstances of the present and immersing in the textures of a different life.

Lately, I've begun to think of this as the touchstone of a quiet revolution, an idea as insurrectionary, in its own sense, as those of Thomas Paine. Reading, after all, is an act of resistance in a landscape of distraction, a matter of engagement in a society that seems to want nothing more than for us to disengage.

It connects us at the deepest levels; it is slow, rather than fast. That is its beauty and its challenge: in a culture of instant information, it requires us to pace ourselves. What does it mean, this notion of slow reading? Most fundamentally, it returns us to a reckoning with time. In the midst of a book, we have no choice but to be patient, to take each thing in its moment, to let the narrative prevail. Even more, we are reminded of all we need to savor—this instant, this scene, this line. We regain the world by withdrawing from it just a little, by stepping back from the noise, the tumult, to discover our reflections in another mind. As we do, we join a broader conversation, by which we both transcend ourselves and are enlarged. In the *Tao Te Ching*, Lao Tse observes, "The whirlwind's spent before the morning ends; / The storm will pass before the day is done. / Who made them, wind and storm? Heaven and earth. / If heaven itself cannot storm for long, / What matter, then, the storms of man?" Twenty-five hundred years after he lived and died, I read those lines and feel connected—to the author and his words. It is in this way that reading becomes an act of meditation, with all of meditation's attendant difficulty and grace. I sit down. I try to make a place for silence. It's harder than it used to be, but still, I read.

AFTERWORD

I wrote *The Lost Art of Reading* in 2010. The book grew out of an essay I had published the previous summer in the *Los Angeles Times*, where I was then book editor, and sought to express—and to reckon with—an encroaching distraction I had begun to notice during the presidential election of 2008. This distraction had manifested itself as an inability to concentrate, particularly when I was reading, to set the noise, the warp and woof of the culture, aside. I don't want to label this anxiety a public one exactly, although that was part of it. Rather, for me at the time, the problem felt more like atomization, a push and pull between my outer and inner worlds. On the one hand, there was information, the endless stream of it, pouring out across the internet in a cascade of bytes and data. On the other, my humanity. I had begun to lose sight of the latter, I came to believe, by virtue of the overwhelming presence of the former, the constant pull of email, texts, social media, and a 24/7 news cycle, in which to turn away even for an hour felt a lot like getting lost. Nearly a decade later, I am here to tell you, it is better and it is worse.

As for better, *The Lost Art of Reading* did what I'd hoped it might. Somehow, it allowed me to find my way back to the page. I don't want to say that my distraction disappeared, because it hasn't. At the same time, I learned (or relearned) how to make a space for silence and for stillness, how to turn towards the world by, in a sense, turning away. I compartmentalized, protecting both my time to be distracted and my time to concentrate. I became a reader again. And not a moment too soon, because we are worse off than we were in 2010. We are more divided, more divisive; we live inside the psychodrama of a disruptive would-be king. The reality is that it's impossible to keep up. I am writing this in February 2018, in a nation that feels to me as if it is coming apart at the seams. But maybe this is the calm before the storm. Who knows where we will be in six months? Who knows where we will be this afternoon? I write to the president on Twitter. I talk about him all day, every day. Distraction? No, it's worse than that: not distraction but full-on dislocation. I am reporting back to you from inside a catastrophe, and I have no idea how it will or won't (d)evolve. You may read this now, or you may read it in a dozen, two dozen years. You may see this moment, the moment we now occupy, through the soft lens of hindsight. Or you may be embroiled in a crisis that makes the current one look like preamble, John Winthrop's shining city on a hill. I don't know; I can't say. All I can do is remain present, think for myself, be here now. All I can do is tell it as I experience it: this is how it is; this is how we are.

And yet, I am not without hope, not without spirit, although some days such a posture, it is difficult. We remain, in spite of everything—the gerrymandering and the hacking and the voter suppression—a democracy, as we saw in Alabama and Virginia in 2017. We have the right, the *obligation*, to vote and organize. I'm not trying to write a stump speech, but if I were, this is what I'd say. In California and Wisconsin, Pennsylvania and Ohio and New York, we have no choice but to try to find some way to come together, if we don't want to continue to be split apart.

So what do we do? Same as ever: we put our shoulders to the wheel. We help in whatever way is available to us, from each according to his or her abilities, to each according to his or her needs. We afflict the comfortable and comfort the afflicted. We behave as human beings. In part, that means making space to advocate;

in part, it means standing up and speaking out. "If you are a bystander," Abbie Hoffman once insisted, "you are not innocent." This is especially so in a time when, as Yeats wrote, "the best lack all conviction, while the worst / Are full of passionate intensity." What I am describing is a revolution of sensibility. We refuse to normalize by, in part, maintaining *our* sense of what is normal—as an act not of forgetting but of remembering. I am an American patriot, although I understand this is a loaded phrase. What I mean is that I believe in what we could be, even as I see us as we are. You can call that bifurcation, but I prefer to think of it as double vision, in which two opposing or unreconciled ideas coexist in my head at the same time.

On January 20, 2017, the evening of the inauguration, I went to a small theater on the campus of the University of Southern California, where a recital version of the opera *Hopscotch* was to be performed. For those who don't know it, *Hopscotch* is a love story loosely inspired by Julio Cortázar's 1963 novel of the same name; it was first staged—if that's the word for it— during the fall of 2015 by performers riding with small audience clusters in twenty-four cars. The intent (or one of them) was to activate the streets of Los Angeles as public space. Los Angeles has long had an ambivalent relationship to its streets; it is a built environment developed around the ideal of the single-family home. In that sense, *Hopscotch* presents both an aesthetic and a social challenge: asking, requiring even, that we consider art, or narrative, as a public act. If the streets themselves can be a landscape for creativity, they can be a landscape for anything, an idea encoded into the structure of the piece.

Something similar, it might be said, unfolded in the wake of the inauguration: art as quiet protest, a reclamation of aesthetic faith. Part of the reimagining *Hopscotch* demands is that of the *dérive*, the situationist strategy for dislocation, in which the map of one city is superimposed over the streets of another, forcing us to encounter familiar landscapes fresh. Do I need to say that this is also a metaphor of sorts for our political climate? In such a disconnected landscape, I want to believe art affords us certain answers or at least a shared experience. We come together through the movement of the work, through our immersion, and when it is finished, we feel, for a moment anyway, less alone. That's what happened in that recital hall full of people frankly frightened of the future. I sat with friends, although I had not known they would be there; to find them in that audience was like discovering a passage home. Before the performance, Yuval Sharon, who conceived and directed *Hopscotch*, offered a few contextual notes. "I pledge allegiance," he told us, "to a vision of art as a communal activity because this too has its utopian function . . . For when the lost part of our souls can find its voice in a communal setting, inspired by the cooperative work of a large and diverse group of individuals, then perhaps we can find the strength as individuals and as a community to rise to the challenges that now face us. For when everything that made up our identity seems under attack, art can remind us what it is we are called to fight for, namely our humanity."

This is the point of *Hopscotch*, which is driven, on a certain level, by its own disorientation. But it is also, I want to tell you, the point of everything. Art as communion, art as community, art as (yes) resistance in the sense that it invites or provokes us to complexity. "I can't go on, I'll go on," Samuel Beckett famously observed, and if this has long felt to me like a code for living, it is only more so now, at a time and place where, as it has ever been, what happens next is up to us.

ABOUT THE AUTHOR

DAVID L. ULIN is the author or editor of ten books, including *Sidewalking: Coming to Terms with Los Angeles*, shortlisted for the PEN/Diamonstein-Spielvogel Award for the Art of the Essay, and the Library of America's *Writing Los Angeles: A Literary Anthology*, which won a California Book Award. The former book editor and book critic of the *Los Angeles Times*, he is the recipient of a Guggenheim Foundation Fellowship, a Tom and Mary Gallagher Fellowship from Black Mountain Institute at the University of Nevada, Las Vegas, and a Lannan Residency Fellowship.